Stories of an

EVERYDAY PILGRIM

ESTHER HIZSA

Stories of an Everyday Pilgrim
Copyright © 2015 Esther Hizsa
All rights reserved.

Printed and bound by CreateSpace in the United States of America

Except when noted, all Scripture quotations are from the HOLY BIBLE, NEW INTERNATIONAL VERSION copyright© 2011 by Biblica.

"Welcoming Prayer" is excerpted from The Contemplative Life Program 40 Day Practice WELCOMING PRAYER Copyright© 2005 Contemplative Outreach, Ltd. All Rights Reserved. Authors and Editors: Gail Fitzpatrick-Hopler, Pamela Gursoy, and Timothy Koock. Owner: Contemplative Outreach, Ltd. 10 Park Place, 2nd Floor, Suite B, Butler, NJ 07450.

Every person in this book is real. In order to protect their privacy and preserve our relationships, I have not always used their given names and have altered some details. Other details, that may seem hard to believe, have not been changed. They actually happened.

Cover design by Fred & Esther Hizsa and Jeremy & Heidi Braacx
Cover photograph by Michael Beales
Author photograph by Fred Hizsa

Library and Archives Canada Cataloguing in Publication

Hizsa, Esther, 1957-, author
Stories of an everyday pilgrim / Esther Hizsa.

ISBN 978-1-5146-7531-1 (paperback)

1. Christian life. 2. God (Christianity). I. Title.

BV4501.3.H58 2015   248.4   C2015-906367-1

Visit *An Everyday Pilgrim* at www.estherhizsa.com

*For the handsome fellow
also known as,
Fred*

CONTENTS

Foreword iv
1. A Heart Set On Pilgrimage 1
2. Pilgrimage 3
3. The Right Place 4
4. In the Shelter of God's Wings 6
5. Easter Saturday 9
6. Resurrection 12
7. Receiving the Kingdom 14
8. Gracie 18
9. Open 21
10. Tapestry 23
11. Wide-Open Spaces 24
12. November Rain 26
13. Telling the Truth 28
14. The Waiting Room 32
15. Gentle Jesus 35
16. God in the Dark: Theory 38
17. God in the Dark: Practice 41
18. A Disturbing Solution to Poverty 44
19. Witnessing Glory 46
20. The Labyrinth 49
21. A Home for Everyone 52
22. Giving Birth to My Feelings 55

23. Patron Saint of the Perpetually Annoyed 57
24. Seasons...60
25. In Martha's Defense...62
26. On the Eighth Day God Painted My Office.......65
27. Peace, Be Still..69
28. The Girl by the Door 71
29. Stretching More Than the Heavens....................74
30. Train Wreck...78
31. Being Here...81
32. Headwinds...83
33. Astronomical Units..86
34. Enough Compassion 89
35. Serious Business 92
36. Engaging in Serious Business 96
37. Trust Me 99
38. Pillars of Salt... 102
39. Reason to Pause... 105
40. Open My Eyes... 107
41. What My Body Knows.................................... 110
42. Branches Wide and Open 113
43. Legless in a Dumpster..................................... 116
44. Peace Dancing 118
45. Half.. 121
46. Surfin' USA 124
47. Let Go.. 127
48. Something Extra.. 130
49. A Voice on the Periphery................................ 132
50. Necessary Commas... 134
51. A Painless Death 136
52. Really Useful Engines..................................... 139

53. Come Down 141
54. The Divine Revelation of Sin 144
55. Felix Culpa! 146
56. Christ, the Sin-Bearer 149
57. The Evil Side of Pies 152
58. Weeds of Insecurity 154
59. Gifts 157
60. Notice What You Notice 159
61. Holy Indifference 162
62. Stones 164
63. A Still Small Voice 165
64. Beginning Again 169
65. Water 172
66. Gathered Home 173
67. Water II 176
68. Journey's End 177

FOREWORD

AWARENESS AND LOVING ENCOUNTER anchor a pilgrim's journey. Awareness in the details of life leads to intimate encounter with God in all of it.

Our contemplative journeys take us outside the boundaries of what we often think of as religious or even spiritual. They open us up to discover God lovingly at work everywhere. We see that in the Gospels, as people welcomed Jesus into their situations and experienced his transforming love. We see that in our own lives, which are also rich with moments of awareness and encounter. And I have seen that in Esther's life.

Stories of an Everyday Pilgrim powerfully illustrates the importance of paying attention to our life. I don't think I have ever known someone more clear about the working of God in their life. Since we first met in 2003, I have had the privilege of knowing Esther within the many facets of our shared partnership in SoulStream. She is knowledgeable and open, willing to risk, and willing to be led into new territory of the soul.

Esther's stories demonstrate these same delightful qualities in a stunning way. Her writing is consistent with her life as we all know her, and that is what makes the book weighty with integrity. Gradually she provides us compelling accounts of how she has been carried from fear, uncertainty, and a driven need to perform well and be good into the wide expanse of God's tender love for her.

Her journey is deceptively simple. They are just stories of an everyday person after all. But don't read them quickly. They cry out to be savored. Each is like a secret tunnel to something extraordinarily profound and heart-warming.

Enjoy this book! Let Esther be a trustworthy guide to you, sensitizing you to the tender moments of your own everyday life. And trust the Spirit to use the power of these stories to take you into deep and surprising encounters with God's ever-present love for you wherever you may be.

—Jeff Imbach

Jeff Imbach, the founding president of the Henri Nouwen Society of Canada, also co-founded SoulStream Initiatives and facilitates SoulStream courses. A long-time pastor in Calgary, Jeff has offered spiritual direction for thirty years. He is the author of two books: The Recovery of Love: Christian Mysticism and the Addictive Society, *and the award-winning,* The River Within: Loving God, Living Passionately.

Give thanks to the Beloved
with your whole heart;
tell the story of Love's way.
—Psalm 9:1
Nan C. Merrill, *Psalms for Praying: An Invitation to Wholeness*

1. A HEART SET ON PILGRIMAGE

SATURDAY MORNINGS MY MOTHER used to pile us into the car and drive to town. While my older brother and sister had accordion lessons, Mom took my little brother and me shopping. Our favorite store, the only one I clearly remember, was the European delicatessen.

I can still see the grooves in the worn wooden floor and Swiss chocolate lined up next to jars of fruit-flavored candies. Wedges of cheese were displayed behind glass, and dried sausages hung from the ceiling. The smells—oh the aromas—that teased me as I watched thin pieces of salami fall from the slicer, and as I opened the bin of crusty buns. Finally, back at the car, my mom reached into the brown paper bag she carried and handed me a bun.

"Wait here," she said and took my brother with her to fetch our siblings. You could do that in those days. No one thought twice about leaving a five-year-old alone for a few minutes.

Too nice a day to sit in the car, I leaned against it and dug out the middle of my bun. After I stuck it on my thumb and finished it off, I didn't know what to do with myself, so I put one hand on a light post and swung around it. I sang, "Jesus loves me this I know, for the Bible tells me so."

As I sang, the words twirled with me, and I forgot I was waiting to go home. I felt like I had already come home to Someone big and important, and that Someone loved me. All the voices that told me otherwise flew far, far away. I knew what I knew.

Wait with me, God said. I heard the invitation again and again throughout my life, and sometimes I lingered with God, but most times I didn't. I had too many things to do.

At forty-eight I was finishing a theology degree when a friend told me he had spent six hours alone with God and Henri Nouwen's *The Way of the Heart*. When I heard how my friend was both shaken and taken by the experience, I wanted to go and be with God too. Yet I had responsibilities of a job and family and assignments due. How could I possibly get away? But when I accidentally deleted one of my essays, I knew I needed a break. "You can't give what you haven't got," a preacher from Ghana once repeated a dozen times in the same sermon.

"I'm thinking of going to Rivendell," I said to my husband, Fred. "Just overnight. What do you think?"

"That sounds like a good idea," he said. "Would you like me to drive you to the ferry?"

A few days later, I carried my backpack up Cates Hill on Bowen Island to Rivendell Retreat Centre. I opened Nouwen's little book and read, prayed, and waited in the silence. For the first time, I prayed without words and simply rested in God.

"You look different," Fred said when he picked me up the next day.

I felt different. My heart was set on pilgrimage. God was calling me to explore the height, depth and breadth of what I knew when I was five: Jesus loves me.

> *Blessed are those whose strength is in you,*
> *whose hearts are set on pilgrimage.*
> —Psalm 84:5

2. PILGRIMAGE

Ash Wednesday
he's on the road
    waiting for me

today we begin
a forty-day walk
to Jerusalem

I lace up my shoes
and follow
    from a safe distance

but it's bound to happen
his eyes will catch mine
and I must summon the courage
    not to look away

for in his loving gaze
questions arise
    memories
    hopes
    and fears

and we will
carry them all
    to Jerusalem

3. THE RIGHT PLACE

THE TOPIC IN MY Systematic Theology class was creation. Playing the atheist, the professor invited us to convince him that God exists. In reference to Psalm 19:1, he asked, "How do the heavens declare the glory of God? I don't hear any voices calling, 'Glory to God! Glory to God!'"

Many students presented their arguments. With a wink and a smile, he commended but dismissed each attempt. Then I remembered a book I had read for the class, *Miracles* by C. S. Lewis. In it Lewis said artists often include something unusual in their work that functions as their signature. Creation is God's art and miracles are God's signature. I thought: if artwork declares the glory of the artist, then God's artwork—creation—declares God's glory. I had an answer, but was it *the* answer?

"It's simply this," the professor said. "Nature is an artifact, something tangible God made. In the same way artwork declares the glory of the artist, creation declares the glory of God."

Agony. It was the right answer. I had a chance to fit into the pious pecking order, and I blew it.

When I finally put away my flagellate, I noticed the professor had turned from his notes. He leaned an elbow on the lectern, laced his fingers together and said, "As important as it is to have sound theology—and it is important. Who was it that said, 'A mist in the pulpit, produces fog in the pews'? Charles Spurgeon?—nevertheless, be careful. It's possible to leave this college knowing a great deal about God, without actually knowing God. You can learn all about prayer and forget to pray. And that would be a tragedy."

The next morning I was prompted to avoid tragedy and prayed. As I breathed in the solitude, I thought of yesterday's class. I felt a flutter in my chest. I am God's art, an artifact that testifies to God's glory. I have been divinely created and declared good.

Before delight took root, I began to despair. God, have I ruined your art? Have I distorted your work so much that your signature's illegible? How do I begin to recover your original handiwork? And it's not only a renewing of my mind that I need. It's my head, heart, soul—and my body too.

As I sat overwhelmed by the hugeness of it all, I realized that I was overwhelmed in the right place: in prayer with my Maker.

I sat for a moment and a picture formed in my mind. I saw myself as a child, and Jesus had walked in and caught me playing with God's paints. Horrified that I had messed things up, I handed Jesus the brush. But he didn't take it; he took me. He picked me up and held me. We were nose to nose, and his eyes were filled with me.

It doesn't really matter what happened after that. If I told you that he looked under my arm for God's signature (tickling me in the process), you'd likely think I was making it up. But you don't need a theology degree to know that's the sort of thing Jesus would do.

4. IN THE SHELTER OF GOD'S WINGS

I MEDITATE ON PSALM 91 and imagine myself in the shelter of God's wings, resting in the shadow of the Almighty. Angels relieve me of my duties. I can hang up the worries of my day, click off my brain, and rest.

Be still, I tell myself, close your eyes and savor the rest.

Seconds later my eyes are open, my body tense. I can't stop thinking about my son, Rudy. He hurt his ankle at work and has hobbled around for days. How can I get him to go to the doctor?

I need to get up. I'm overheating in these feathers. I need to—

"Let it go. You need to rest," says a voice.

Yes. I have come to rest in God's delicate down, to be still and pray.

As I feel myself relax again, I wonder if the Good Samaritan was praying on his way from Jerusalem to Jericho. Maybe that's why he saw the injured man.

I can't believe it. I'm lying here in the shadow of God's wings thinking of my next sermon. Oh well, maybe I should get up and write this down.

"No sermon writing!" says the same gravelly voice I heard earlier.

This voice isn't God's. It's the angel sitting next to me—and I swear he's just smoked a cigarette. He lowers his newspaper slightly. I see his pale blue eyes and unshaved cheeks. "Rest." He wags his forefinger at me. "That's all God wants you to do right now. Rest."

He raises the sports section against my objections. I lie back down and blow off the feather that tickles my upper lip. Beads of sweat collect on the bridge of my nose. These wings feel like a straightjacket.

The angel lowers his newspaper again. "Beginning is always hard. Let the thoughts wash over you. It'll get easier."

But it doesn't. Acidic bile springs into my throat. A sudden cramp makes me hug my knees to my chest. "What's going on? I feel like I'm in a detox ward," I tell him.

"In a way you are," he says.

"What? I thought I came here to pray. Why would I need to dry out? I've never had more than two glasses of wine in an evening. Never done drugs. What do I need to detox from?"

"Your compulsive thoughts," he answers. "Everybody's got them. You're so used to them, you don't realize how much they run your life."

"I'm here in the shadow of God's wings to detoxify my brain?"

"More or less."

"This is prayer?" I tighten the grip on my knees against a second wave of cramps.

A female angel enters to relieve her colleague. "My goodness, it reeks in here," she says to him. "How can you stand it?" The new angel brushes past me and yanks open a window. She inhales deeply. The cool air makes the perspiration on my neck tingle. She introduces herself and sits down, crossing one leg over the other. She wears support hose and a crisp white uniform.

"You're doing fine. You've been praying for what? Seven and a half minutes, nearly eight? Give God five or ten more, and you'll be surprised by what our Lord does with it."

I wait a while longer. The no-nonsense angel crosses her arms and taps her forefinger on one elbow. She watches my distractions emerge, taunt me, and then leave. One look from her tells them they are not welcome to return. When the last one departs, so does she, quietly closing the door behind her.

Finally I am alone with soft feathers and silence. In the solitude I hear God's heart beating. Or is it mine? Or is it both? We are connected by a wordless umbilical cord.

This is prayer?

This is prayer.

5. EASTER SATURDAY

IT'S AWKWARD BEING VOCATIONALLY challenged while my friends prepare for retirement. I've just graduated and people keep asking what I plan to do with my theology degree. I say, "Be a pastor, I guess."

I guess. It's not clear to me. A year ago I left the denomination that I belonged to since I was born—a denomination, by the way, that ordains women. Now I'm attending a church that doesn't want a woman pastor. I'm in a temporary church, a temporary place between a death and a resurrection.

Last week I was filling in for a minister in another church who was on vacation. My family and I parked in the Minister Reserved parking spot. I sat at the minister's desk, put on my glasses, and looked over the bulletin.

"You look like you belong there," my daughter, Heidi, said. After the service people shook my hand warmly, thanked me for coming, and said I'd make a great pastor. Everyone's so sure of my calling.

I was as well until I took a course called Christian Imagination. The big assignment in that class was to produce something artistic. For me that meant writing. Ever since I was young, I've kept a journal and enjoyed writing poems, songs and stories. But twelve years ago, when Fred became too ill to work, I needed to stop playing with words and get a job.

What a coincidence! Our church happened to need someone to run their children and youth ministries. I was an answer to prayer. No training required (no one else wanted the job). I donned my Super Christian costume, tuned my radio to the teen station, and took off to save the day. In the endless marathon of Capture the Flag, kid's crafts, mission trips, meetings, and phone calls, I forgot I was ever an artist.

That was my life until the Christian Imagination class introduced me to the works of Flannery O'Connor and Madeleine L'Engle. Both women found my buried treasure and held up diamonds and emeralds saying, "Your stories are priceless. Believe it. Write them." Not only did I get to write the story that had been percolating in me, I got to write it for credit. It was as if someone put a plate of chocolate brownies in front of me and said, "Eat as many as you like, and I'll pay you to eat them."

I recommitted my life to writing. But two stories later, my enthusiasm dried up like a rootless seed on a gravel road. Although my school work was demanding, it was the church that was choking me. It was a mess. I stopped writing for pleasure and wrote for survival, pouring misery into my journal. I wanted to save the church, but it wouldn't be saved. And though they loved me dearly, the church couldn't save me either. I was an unfortunate casualty.

That was a year ago. Since then I have been in an in-between place that feels like the Saturday between Good Friday and Easter Sunday. I buried Esther, the youth and children's pastor and now await the resurrection of another me.

When I worked with teens, I reminded them that we are not defined by what we do but by who we are in Christ. I knew that—or thought I did—until my job ended, and then I was nobody.

I felt like a kid being left out of the in-crowd at noon hour. I sobbed like a seven-year-old. I wanted Jesus to make the church people play nicely. But adults don't get noon hour monitors to make life fair.

Life was extremely unfair on Good Friday when they crucified an innocent man. But before his grand re-entrance, the world had to live through Easter Saturday, the one day in history when Jesus was dead.

On that gray Saturday, the disciples were pierced with images—Jesus gasping for breath, jackals throwing dice for his clothes, and Mary wailing, rocking on the edge of despair. Yet that same day, angels were tuning up their harps for a great celebration. They were whispering excitedly among themselves, "Poor disciples, poor Mary. Don't they know? God will turn their mourning into dancing and remove their sackcloth and clothe them with joy." Resurrection was just around the corner. All they had to do was wait. It must have been the longest day of their lives.

This has been the longest day of my life, and I don't even know if it's noon yet. There's nothing to do but wait, wait for the Lord to come and save me.

I don't know how to do that. Like many Christians, after I "got saved," I proceeded to spend the rest of my life saving myself. But when the ultimate sacrifice has been made and salvation accomplished, there's no point in constructing a self-improvement plan. It would be like trying to move a mountain of sand with a spoon when God is about to show up with a front-end loader.

I wait for the Holy Loader. I wait impatiently, more than night watchmen wait for the dawn.

> *I wait for the LORD, my whole being waits,*
> *and in his word I put my hope.*
> *I wait for the Lord*
> *more than watchmen wait for the morning,*
> *more than watchmen wait for the morning.*
> —Psalm 130:5, 6

6. RESURRECTION

my world has been torched
every bit of it
blistered and charred

ambiguity grates my soul
I can't separate
    fire from backfire
    grief from guilt
nothing is pure
not even my resentment

    just give me one sip of hope

I spot my cup in the rubble
but all that is left is the handle
I stare at it
and weep
to death

mourners
toss handfuls of words
in my grave

days
weeks
months pass

then one day
I feel cold
I feel
a worn out cliché
poking me in the back

God is good

I roll it around in my cupped hand
and wonder
what to do with it

7. RECEIVING THE KINGDOM

THE GREY-HAIRED NUN welcomed me into her living room of pink, lilac, and moss green. I tucked my bicycle helmet under a chair and sat across from her in the morning sunlight—me in shorts and a jersey and she in a navy gabardine dress.

"Tell me why you've come for spiritual direction." She folded her hands on her lap.

"I have this theology degree, and I'm not sure what God wants me to do with it. I thought I knew but . . ."

"Why don't you tell me a bit about yourself."

"My husband and I have a son and daughter, both adults now. Last month I finished my Master of Divinity degree at Regent College, and I work weekends as a sleepover residential care worker with developmentally disabled adults."

She wanted to know more. I told her that Fred had been ill with kidney disease until my brother donated one of his kidneys. I told her about the church our family had attended since our kids were preschoolers. "For years I worked there overseeing the children and youth ministries," I said. Then I told her the unfair reasons why I left.

"And the church you attend now?" she asked.

"I don't know if I fit in—as a leader, I mean. The church is looking for a new pastor, and they keep referring to the prospective candidate as 'him.' I try to convince them that the right man for the job could be a woman."

"You?"

"Oh no. I don't want that much responsibility. I just don't like it when women are treated unfairly, so I speak up."

"Sounds like you've been speaking up for a long time."

A tear pooled and slid down my cheek.

After a pause she asked, "What do you like doing in your spare time?"

"Riding my bike and writing," I said, offering two more puzzle pieces to the mismatched jumble on her lap.

Near the end of the hour, she asked, "Why do you think you have to do anything with your degree?"

Her question surprised me. "People expect me to pastor a church."

"People? Well, these people don't know you well."

A slight tremor shot up into my throat: I am one of those people.

She went on. "How would it be, for a while anyway, if you kept attending this church but don't try to change anything?"

I folded my arms. "So, no getting involved in the decision making . . ."

"And don't analyze the sermons. Go and receive whatever God has for you."

"Yeah. I suppose I could do that."

"And how would it be, for a while anyway, if you kept your night job, and spent your days writing?"

"That would be heavenly."

"How do you feel when you think about it?"

"Relieved."

"Yes." She clasped her hands together and leaned forward. "What you call 'relief' is peace. Perhaps you haven't known it for a while."

The sister gave me a hug and invited me to come back and see her again. I biked home along the Fraser River, savoring the peace I felt.

After that visit, whenever I thought about becoming a full-time pastor, I noticed an uncomfortable gnawing in my throat. Still, I longed to be in leadership and preach. Regularly I checked online ads from various churches that were looking to hire a pastor. Nothing called out to me.

In the meantime, I joined a writers' group, traded in my old clunker of a bike for a new one, and spent Sunday mornings at church sitting and listening.

That fall I returned for spiritual direction.

"You look rested and happy," the sister said.

"I guess I am."

She lit a candle and invited me to become aware of God's presence in the silence. "Begin whenever you're ready," she said.

"The church hired a new pastor," I told her. "A man of course. A few months after he arrived, he said he wanted to get to know Fred and me. So we had him over for lunch. He asked me about my experiences in ministry and my passions. I told him how I longed for God's people to be a community. And I told him I loved writing and being involved in the arts worship service we had."

The nun nodded and waited for me to continue.

"Then I asked him what he thought about women being pastors."

"And?"

"He said he doesn't have a problem with it. And—you won't believe this—last week he offered me a part-time position as associate pastor."

"What will you be doing?"

"Help new people get connected, organize arts worship services, and preach."

"Sounds perfect!"

"It's a princess job. I get to do everything I like, and I still have time to write."

"And what did you do to make it happen?"

I had to think about that for a minute. "Nothing," I said.

"God gave it to you?"

"Yeah. I assume when I don't do anything, nothing happens."

But God was doing something. God was speaking up for me.

*Do not be afraid, little flock,
for your Father has been pleased to give you the kingdom.*
—Luke 12:32

8. GRACIE

Keep me as the apple of your eye;
hide me in the shadow of your wings
from the wicked who are out to destroy me,
from my mortal enemies who surround me.
—Psalm 17:8, 9

I LOVE RIDING MY bicycle, especially on long empty roads. I picture myself in the shadow of God's wings as I pedal along to the beat of God's heart. I hope the Holy Spirit will speak to me, but often God is silent. I would doubt God was ever there except for the thoughts that are left behind. I find them later in conversations when I hear myself say, "I was riding my bike when I realized something." Then I write that "something" in my journal. I want to ride and pray for miles.

I used to think all bikes were relatively the same until Heidi got a job selling them. "Mom, your bike is too big for you," she said. "And feel how heavy it is? If you tried a road bike, you'd love it."

Two months later we found Gracie in a funky bike shop in North Vancouver. Heidi pointed to the sky-blue road bike hanging from the ceiling: a seventeen inch women-specific Trek 1500 on sale for *only* $1350. A young salesman in baggy shorts and sandals got it down, checked it over, and told me that I could take it out for a spin. Half an hour later I returned. The fat grin on my face said it all.

At first I referred to Gracie as my pocket-bike; she was that small and light. But after the store mechanic fit her frame to mine and I snapped my new shoes into her pedals, I felt like we were one. That meant she needed more than a description: she needed a name.

I didn't name her after Gracie Slick although she is slick, especially with her Kevlar tires. The rubber on them is so smooth they look naked, as if I'm riding on inner tubes. No, I chose Gracie because grace is what I need when I clip into her pedals and ride in the city. If I don't unclip in time, a sudden stop becomes an instant fall. I fell down four times the first week I got my new bike. To avoid a fifth, I went back to using regular pedals and running shoes.

Even then I continued to rely on grace. I felt nervous riding down steep hills. Trucks squeezed me to the curb. Dogs barked from the back of pickups, and drivers, cell phones in hand, cut in front of me without signaling.

And Gracie has a shadow side. Her components are expensive, her upkeep demanding, and then there's the skintight spandex she expects me to wear.

As if this wasn't enough, one more thing bothered me and made me regret spending so much money on a bike. Sometimes when I finally got out for a ride and opened my mind in prayer, the day's events flooded in uncensored and sideswiped me. I suppose I believed that the more I rode and prayed, the more holy my thought-life would become. I was wrong.

One Sunday evening I rode to the group home where I worked. After-church conversations rattled me. I recalled feeling discounted by one person and judged by another. And there were at least four stupid things I wished I'd never said. Like wicked enemies, these memories seemed "out to destroy me." For eight long miles, they violated my sacred space. I couldn't ride fast enough to escape them.

I griped at God, I thought getting this bike was your idea. Obviously not.

Maybe I should take it back.

Just before ten o'clock, I parked Gracie inside the front door of the East Vancouver town house shared by five women—each with a developmental disability. My shift began the way it always did.

"Who is it?" Helen sang out.

"It's me, Esther."

"Why didn't you bring your car?"

"My husband took it to work."

"Oh." She pushed back her grey bangs and said, "You're cute."

"You're cute too."

After the evening staff left, Helen watched me make the pullout couch into a bed. The mattress flopped down creating a gust of air and she giggled. Then she hugged me goodnight and headed upstairs. Soon I heard her distinctive snore.

I turned my back on Gracie and her feigned innocence, and climbed into bed. Rest caressed my body. It gathered up my thoughts in the silence.

You can let go, I sensed the Holy Spirit say. *You don't need to figure it out.*

In a wakeful moment in the middle of the night, I realized Gracie was too scuffed up to return. I was stuck with her.

9. OPEN

DURING MY BIBLE READING one morning, Psalm 95 invited me to pray.

"Come," wooed the psalmist, "let us sing; let us shout. Let us come before God with thanksgiving."

"Come," he called again, "let us kneel before the Lord, our maker."

"Come," a chorus echoed, "for he is our God and we are the people of his pasture."

I imagined myself worshipping with angels. Violins, cellos and tympani approached a crescendo and—

Suddenly, at the end of verse seven, my sweet psalmist turned into a finger-pointing prophet. This killjoy pounded his staff on the ground and glared at me. "Today, if you hear his voice, do not harden your heart as you did in Meribah."

When was the last time I was in Meribah? Hmm. Let me think.

The psalmist raised an eyebrow at my cynicism. "Many praise the glory of God, but few let our glorious God speak. Now don't give me the I-would-never-do-that look. As soon as you have a bit of silence you fill it with something."

I knew he meant something like solitaire. The other day the house was too quiet. I had clicked on game 701 of computer solitaire when Rudy dropped by to get his mail.

"Hey, Mom. Taking a break?"

"Yeah." I felt a twinge of guilt. "It's a brain blocker."

After he left I resisted the temptation to select game 702. But I was restless. I didn't want to think about the uncomfortable feelings that emerged in the silence.

I suppose the Holy Spirit would speak through these feelings if I was receptive enough. This is my theory based on the fact that the Spirit is quite articulate when my feelings overwhelm me. I can't shut them out forever. Eventually the dam bursts and I am flooded by a level five Tsunami. Then I find myself alone on an emotional rooftop and very attentive to God's voice.

I read somewhere: we are what we do with our silence. Back in Psalm 95, verse eight to be exact, the Psalmist chewed me out for using the silence to build walls around my heart.

"Do that," this prophet warned, "and you'll forfeit rest."

"Okay, okay. I get it."

I shut off the computer, sat back and took hold of the silence. I listened for God's voice. I felt relaxed, but my hands were clenched like they are at the dentist's. I opened them and a Bruce Cockburn song came to mind.

Open, open.

How the Spirit enfolded me when I first heard that song!

Open, the Spirit sang to my heart, *open.*

Once again I opened myself to the silence and waited.

The clock ticked louder on the down stroke than the up. A bird chirped outside. Thoughts drifted in and out.

Twenty minutes later I got up and headed to the shower. The warm water poured over my head and onto my body like a blessing. Joy ignited in my chest and infused me with peace. Then the silence of God welled up in me—and hushed the finger-pointing prophet.

10. TAPESTRY

my life is full of
    knots and hanging
    threads

but when I pray
—when I let

    you

pray in me—
you turn my tapestry over

    peace appears
    horizon hues
in warp and weft

11. WIDE-OPEN SPACES

FRED AND I LOADED our bikes onto the car and headed to the Fraser Valley to ride in its wide-open spaces. We weren't gone five minutes when I began to feel uneasy. Why? What was wrong? Yes, I was preaching on Sunday and this was Thursday, but there was no need to worry. I had prayed and worked hard enough. Now my sermon, like a good wine, needed time to breathe.

Before long anxiety pestered me again, as if it were a petulant creature kicking the back of my seat. I imagined myself confronting it.

"What's your problem?" I demanded.

It shrugged empty-handed.

"Well then, pipe down," I told it.

In the end my sermon was fine, but a month later, anxiety showed up again on our vacation. When it did, I tried to figure out what I needed to worry about. A forgotten item? We could buy it or improvise. Plans thwarted? God must have something else in mind. Each time anxiety showed up, its arguments were less and less convincing. I dismissed its outdated news.

On vacation I could easily sidestep anxiety because it was empty-handed, but I suspected it wouldn't be once we got home. Sure enough Fred and I weren't back twenty-four hours before we faced a calamity. Fear ignited worry and propelled me to act, fix, do something, anything—now. But I didn't want to let go of this peace that had gotten hold of me.

Over the next few days, I watched the Holy Spirit work. The Spirit disarmed my fear by reminding me that God was with me and nudged me to pay attention to what God was doing.

Francois Fénelon, an eighteenth century archbishop, wrote, "Peace is the will of God for you in every situation." In *every* situation. Even when anxiety shows up loaded with complicated problems, the Holy Spirit is already there with buckets of peace—world-confusing, heart-comforting, fear-dispelling peace. Even when worry manages to get the best of me, the Spirit slips me some hope and says, *Remember the day when your anxiety was speechless?*

Now don't get me wrong: anxiety can be useful. I want it to holler if we are driving along, and it notices we're about to be beer-trucked. But it needs to stop crying wolf all the time. It needs to know its place, and its place is definitely in the back seat. I can hear it fine from there.

But the Spirit of Peace is welcome up front anytime. My Cool Companion rolls down the window, waves at people in other cars, and finds the best songs on the radio. And when Peace leads the way, I know I'm headed for wide-open spaces.

12. NOVEMBER RAIN

I DREAM MY BED is made and our living room tidy with everything in its place. That's it, a prophetic snapshot of our house in *Better Homes and Gardens*.

Despite my dream, I wake Tuesday morning uninspired. November rain dampens life. Can't bike; the thought of running exhausts me. I overeat. God doles out my sermon in measured doses as Sunday looms.

On Wednesday I attend a monthly meeting of pastors—mostly men—to get to know one another and pray for our city. I take a risk and tell them about my dream. No one says anything.

On Thursday the writers' group gives me feedback on a story I had hoped to publish. "Great story, but there are too many characters," one person says.

"I think it starts in the wrong place," says another.

A third asks, "Who is the protagonist?"

Afterwards I commiserate with a friend who affirms my ability to write. Belief hangs like a scarf I'm not sure how to tie.

On the drive home, I turn on the windshield wipers and lament. Life was so much easier in the summer. Fewer people, fewer demands. More sunshine, more endorphins, more sex. Each day had space. Oh to feel content for weeks at a time.

Sunday's sermon goes well. I love it when I look all right and say things people tell their friends. For a few hours I feel good, but I know it won't be long before I discover my shirt's on inside out, or that the tag is showing—if not today, tomorrow for sure.

On Monday I read Psalm 73. The psalmist tells me that even when I am grieved and bitter, God is still with me. I think about that, and a thought forms in a remote corner of my brain: God is not against me.

13. TELLING THE TRUTH

"'WHEN HE HAD FINISHED speaking with Abraham, God went up from him.'" The young man reading Genesis 17 aloud at our Thursday night Bible study stopped at verse twenty-two. "What does it mean, 'God went up'? Did God go back up to heaven or something?"

I first met this gangly twenty-year-old with short-cropped hair and an eyebrow ring a year before. He came over one day to show Rudy a video of his most recent adventure: tandem skydiving.

"Jumping out of a plane at eight-thousand feet was the most spiritual experience of my life," he told me. "What a high. Ever since I broke up with my girlfriend, I've been so depressed, I haven't even wanted to have sex."

My pastoral training had not prepared me for this raw intersection between faith and life. I told them dinner was ready.

Later Rudy's friend helped clear the table; he thanked me four times for the meal.

"You can come over for dinner every week if you want to," Rudy said. "Sandy, Dave and Evan do, and so do a bunch of my sister's friends. We have supper and then talk about the Bible. Mom explains stuff that's hard to understand."

The skydiver gave me a hug and promised he'd come.

We were studying the gospel of John when he joined us that fall. After we completed John, we ploughed through all twenty-eight chapters of Acts. He asked questions about the Trinity, prayer, demonology, the canon, textual criticism, creation, evolution, Pentecost, and miracles.

He phoned me one afternoon. "Hey Esther, did you hear about the woman who was skydiving, and her chute didn't open? It was on the news. She was pregnant but didn't know it. She survived. She only had minor injuries and didn't lose the baby. Can you believe it? It's a miracle, like those guys did."

"What guys?"

"Those guys in the Bible that healed the lame man in front of the church. That was a miracle, and so is this, right?"

"Yeah, sure."

"I thought so. See you Thursday."

Now, a year later, we were up to the seventeenth chapter of Genesis, and this young man was ticked off with God. "God leaves? He talks to Abraham, and just leaves?" He took a breath, put his hands down on his open Bible, and looked at each of us. "It's like this. I don't believe God exists." He exhaled and closed his Bible. "There. I said it. Now you know."

"How do you explain life?" I asked.

"It's biology. It just happened. Cells mutated and evolved," he replied.

"But someone or some being had to make the cells."

"I don't know. Maybe there was a big explosion."

"But what exploded?" I asked him. "Where did it come from?"

"It was just there."

"But how did it get there? There's too much intelligent life in the universe for it to have happened by chance. That's why many scientists believe in God."

"Well, I don't. He hasn't done anything to make me believe in him." His face was red, and he looked about to cry.

Now I understood. "God was with you," I said gently, "and now it feels like God's gone."

"I don't care," he said.

"God didn't really leave Abraham," Rudy said, "and God hasn't left you either."

"It's the truth," I said. But our friend wasn't willing to jump out of an airplane with God as his parachute. God was too unpredictable, too unreliable.

I can relate to him. Many times I have felt abandoned by God. And to be honest, I can tell the truth easier than I can believe it. Sometimes Jesus' promise to be with us all the time has a hollow ring to it. How could he have made such an unqualified claim? Sure, I believed God was with me sometimes, in extenuating circumstances, but plenty of times I felt alone.

Not long after the skydiver quit coming to our Bible study, I read a book on prayer by Father Thomas Keating, a Benedictine monk. He said, "The chief thing that separates us from God is the thought that we are separated from him. If we get rid of that thought, our troubles will be greatly reduced."[1]

Let me be rid of "that thought," I prayed. I felt stranded on the wrong side of the Jordan, longing for the Promised Land.

That was half a dozen years ago, and since then, I have begun noticing that God is around more than I realized. God keeps leaving proof behind, and I have written about my findings in this book. What I have discovered is that the more I pay attention, the more I notice that God has been there all along. Like the man Jesus healed, I was blind and now I see.

Sadly, I don't see much of the skydiver. Last time I ran into him, he was sitting at a table outside a grocery store. He was about to bite into a sandwich when he saw me. He invited me to sit down and offered to share his lunch. I asked how he was doing, and he told me his business was going well. "But I still don't believe in God," he added.

---

[1] Thomas Keating, *Open Mind, Open Heart*. (Warwick, NY: Amity House, 1986), 44.

I sensed God was there, watching him enjoy his lunch and reassuring me that I didn't need to convince him of anything. I had told the truth; it was up to God to prove it.

14. THE WAITING ROOM

"Could you speak up, please? What seems to be the problem?"

"I'm sick," my twenty-year-old daughter said to the woman behind the Plexiglas.

The emergency nurse moved closer to the microphone and asked, "Any other symptoms?"

"Fever . . . sore throat . . . cough . . ."

Stock questions, minimal answers.

"Take a seat in the waiting room."

Heidi slumped into a chair beside me and leaned her head back against the wall. "I feel lousy." She began to cough again. "What's wrong with me?"

"It's likely the flu, but it's good to get it checked out," I said.

She started to take a deep breath but stopped and covered her nose with her jacket. I smelled it too: a mix of urine, booze, and dirty socks. An unkempt couple dressed in layers of mismatched clothing had wandered in. The man pressed his pockmarked face to the Plexiglas, and then told the floor and ceiling all about his ailments.

The emergency room door opened and closed. Fresh air and cologne. Two broad-shouldered men in matching overcoats and shoes entered. The first one said something to the nurse; the other nodded.

A triage nurse took Heidi's vital signs and directed her to the clerk at Window One. Two ambulance attendants remade a stretcher while Heidi answered more questions. Then the nurse handed Heidi her chart and told her to follow the orange line on the floor to the Emergency Fast Track desk. The line led us past a utility room and more stretchers to another waiting room that smelled as bad as the first.

After the nurse took Heidi to an examination room, I opened *The Cloud of Unknowing*, a book about prayer written by an anonymous Christian mystic in the fourteenth century. I tried to ignore the ambient odors as I read chapter forty-three. It challenged me to "lose the radical self-centered awareness of my being in order to reach the heights of contemplation." According to this mystic, true lovers become oblivious to themselves on account of the one they love. To be united with God, we must learn to forget ourselves.

Now how am I supposed to do that? Wouldn't I have to be aware of myself to know that I was forgetting myself? I closed the book and prayed: Jesus, Son of God, have mercy on me a sinner. But the words sounded like a jingle.

Finally Heidi returned. "It's just a viral infection. If it gets worse, I'm to take this," she said and showed me a prescription for antibiotics.

"Thanks for everything." She hugged me, pressing hot cheek against mine. "Can I come home and sleep in my old room tonight?"

"Of course," I said.

The next morning I stepped over Heidi's sneakers in the hallway. All was well. Coffee in hand, I opened my Bible. The day's readings were heavy: the first passage described the burnt sacrifice offered by the priest, which has an aroma holy and pleasing to God. Psalm 141 picked up the same theme, "May my prayer be set before you like incense; may the lifting up of my hands be like the evening sacrifice."

I offered God my sacrifice of thanks that Heidi was going to be fine. After I confessed my sins, I waited in the silence and hoped God would do something in it. Would I "reach the heights of contemplation"?

I listened to my breathing while a Stellar's jay sang outside my window. Absent-mindedly I opened *The Cloud of Unknowing*. Chapter forty-four was titled, "How a person shall dispose himself so as to destroy the radical self-centered awareness of his being."

Tell me, I asked the mystic skeptically, how do I do that?

The clouded mystic replied, "You must see the depth of your own evil nature and weep."

I closed my eyes again and saw Jesus sitting in a smelly hospital waiting room. I was on his lap—a little girl with my head on his chest. His arms were around me, and I slowly realized the sour odor was coming from the little girl: me.

I recoiled, brushing the image away. When I set my prayer before God "like incense," I wanted God to breathe in gardenias, not the unwashed smell of a prodigal. Thousands of times I have recited the Jesus' prayer asking him to "have mercy on me, a sinner," but I didn't really believe I was one. I skipped from confession to absolution without remorse.

But now sadness ached. It called to me. It clung to my nostrils and led me along an orange line to the One who was waiting for me.

15. GENTLE JESUS

"WHAT'S ON YOUR MIND?" The community health worker sat down on a bench outside our church. She was dressed comfortably in Hawaiian print shorts, a T-shirt, and flip-flops. I wore high heels, a blue print skirt and a black blouse: pretty, but not the best choice for this shadeless, noontime meeting.

"Do you know the woman who plays flute in one of the worship bands?" I asked.

"Long brown hair, early thirties? Nice gal. We've spoken a few times. She put her testimony in the church newsletter a while back. She's pretty open about having a mood disorder."

"She's open about everything, a little too open. People are starting to avoid her. I really like her and want her to feel included in our church community. I've tried a bunch of different things to get her to recognize her alienating behaviors. But nothing seems to help."

"I can see the pickle you're in. Most people don't like having to set boundaries with others. It's got to be tough for them and for her. I'm surprised she still comes to church. I'm glad you're not giving up on her, but you seem to be working awfully hard at this," she said. "Making friends isn't easy—not for me anyway. These things take time."

The sun heated up my dark blouse. Perspiration trickled down my back. Was I more intent on changing this woman than loving her?

I must have sounded like a drill sergeant: Atten-tion! Change now! No excuses. Come on, get with the program.

Shame numbed me as I heard myself end our meeting in a measured monotone. The health worker followed me with her eyes as I got up to go.

"I hope I was some help to you," she said and gave me a hug. "This gal's lucky to have you for a friend."

I nodded blankly and remembered what I heard at a prayer retreat the day before.

"Many of us carry around dysfunctional views of God without even realizing it," the speaker said. He named the most common ones, and I wrote them down: the Distant and Demanding God, the Cosmic Kill-Joy, the Indulgent Grandfather and the Drill Sergeant. After he described each one, he asked if any of these false images of God seemed familiar to us. At the time I didn't think so, but now I realized the Drill Sergeant was alive and well in me.

I walked through the empty parking lot and headed for home, quickening my pace as thoughts jabbed me. How could I have been so insensitive? What was I thinking? My lack of gentleness seemed to be splashed in chilling detail on the front page of my life.

It wasn't until I cycled to work that evening that the real God came to my aid. Gently God folded up the damaging tabloid and pushed the drill sergeant aside. The Spirit reminded me of the last thing the health worker said, and the compassion in her eyes when she said it. I doubted that a regimented god ruled her life, demanding she get things right, bugging her about her weight, or commenting on her looks.

"Be gentle with yourself," the Holy Spirit seemed to say as I climbed into bed that night.

A few days later the flute-player and I sat on the church steps, and I apologized for over functioning.

She laughed. "Don't be hard on yourself. I've learned a few things from you."

"Yeah, well, I wish gentleness was one of them."

"Don't kid yourself, you're nothing compared to my mother. Did I ever tell you about the time . . .?"

> *Take my yoke upon you and learn from me,*
> *for I am gentle and humble in heart,*
> *and you will find rest for your souls.*
> —Matthew 11:29

16. GOD IN THE DARK: THEORY

IT WAS LAB DAY for our spiritual direction class. That meant we took turns giving each other spiritual direction. Our teachers called these sessions "real plays," because we weren't role-playing; we talked about what was really going on in our lives.

"I've tried three times to explain to this woman that there's a problem, and she keeps ignoring me. I hate that," I said when it was my turn to be the directee. "If I confront her, I feel like I'm being too critical; if I don't say anything, I'm afraid it'll happen again."

"How does that make you feel?" my classmate asked.

"Frustrated. A few years ago I never said anything when things bothered me. Now I wonder if I say too much. I don't know what to do."

After a long pause, he asked, "What is it like for you when you don't know what to do?"

My stomach dropped and took my shoulders with it. I struggled to name what I felt. "I feel helpless, I guess."

"Helpless." He let the word sit in front of us. "Tell me what 'helpless' is like."

"Awful. Like I'm stupid or don't matter."

"Was there another time when you felt like this?" he asked.

I thought for a moment. "When I was little, my older brother and sister locked me in the curing room of the cheese factory my dad managed, and I couldn't get out."

"What happened?"

"I panicked. I screamed, but they couldn't hear me because the walls were thick."

"How did you get out?"

"My brother opened the door. Then they laughed at me and said, 'All you had to do was push on the handle.' I felt stupid." I took a tissue from the box on the table beside me and stared at the floor.

"Esther, do you ever experience something like this in your spiritual life?"

"Yes. Often I have a problem to solve and pray for help. But God just stands there and expects me to figure it out myself."

Then I looked up and heard myself declare, "But that's not God! God isn't outside the room laughing. God's inside the room with me."

After I wiped my tears, my classmate asked, "Can you picture Jesus in the room with you?"

I closed my eyes. "He's with me, and I'm a little girl."

"Take some time to be there with him."

At first I saw Jesus near me weeping because, when they shut the door, a wall as thick as the curing room walls went up between us. Then, the next minute, we were outside the room and he said, "Let's go in again." I didn't want to do it, but I let him take my hand and lead me back into the room. This time, when we went in and the door shut, Jesus pulled me onto his lap and said, "Hey, look. I've got a lighter." And he flicked it on. Then he said he kept a ball in there, and we could play with it.

I smiled and explained what I saw. My classmate smiled too, and I felt full.

We prayed, thanking God for this precious revelation of love.

After a moment of silence, our teacher invited us to talk about what we had experienced and observed. Long pauses bracketed each offering; no one wanted to disturb the sense of awe.

Finally my classmate turned to me. "I'm curious," he said. "What are you going to do about that woman that keeps ignoring you?"

"I'll likely say something," I replied, "But at least when I do, I won't hold her responsible for locking me in the curing room."

17. GOD IN THE DARK: PRACTICE

AFTER MY SPIRITUAL DIRECTION session in class, I felt light. That picture of Jesus holding me in the darkness changed everything. He was not outside my problems, living in their solutions, but with me in each and every one of my predicaments. What a marvelous thought to consider during my bike ride home from Abbotsford on a warm evening in June.

Three miles into my ride I got a flat tire. I groaned, turned Gracie upside down and got out a spare inner tube. But the spare wouldn't inflate, and the one that was flat wouldn't hold air long enough for me to find the hole and patch it. I phoned Fred at work. He couldn't think of anything else to do but said he'd call back after he checked the bus routes. I tried inflating the spare tube again and again, but the flat rubber wouldn't respond. The stupid tube didn't seem to care that it was six o'clock, and I was forty miles from home.

I waved at passing cars. The upturned bike and my small stature worked in my favor. The third car stopped. A middle-aged man and his wife were returning home from a wedding. They took me to the bus loop. But when we got there, the bus running west was finished for the day.

The man tapped his finger on the steering wheel while he thought. "If you submerge the tube in water, then you could find the hole."

It was worth a try. I waved goodbye to the couple and headed to a restroom at the gas station across the street. I stuffed a paper towel into the drain hole of the tiny sink and filled it with water while trying to pump up the inner tube and locate the hiss before the tube deflated. Meanwhile Fred phoned a couple of times with more sympathy than advice. Each time I stopped to speak to him, the water drained away and so did my patience.

But the morning's experience was not forgotten. I knew God was with me while I grouched at Fred and got mad at the tube. And I knew God could read my body language which clearly said, Make yourself useful, will you?

Over at the gas pump, a man in his thirties returned the nozzle to its holder and put the gas cap on a new silver pickup. I left Gracie propped up against the restroom door and ran over to plead for a lift.

"We can take you as far as Mount Lehman Road, if that helps," he told me.

"Sure," I replied even though it was only a couple of miles away.

He put the bike in the truck, and I hopped in next to an empty infant car seat.

"You've got a baby," I said to the woman in the passenger seat in front of me.

"A little girl, three months old, and boys, two and five," she replied. "This is the first time my husband and I have been out alone since our daughter was born."

"I'm ruining your date night!"

"Don't give it another thought," she replied.

She thought a cab to Langley would cost twenty bucks. He thought fifty. After he made a few phone calls, we found out he was right.

"That's way too much money," she said. "Why don't we have dinner in Langley?"

"Whatever you say," he replied.

I offered to pay for their gas, but they wouldn't take my money. Neither would the driver of the #501 bus to Surrey Central. He must have observed that one wheel had no tire on it when I secured Gracie to the front of his bus. As soon as I got on board, he handed me a transfer and said, "This one's on me."

The bus meandered through Langley and finally arrived at Surrey Central Skytrain station forty minutes later.

"I've met some kind and generous people today," I said to the driver before the bus came to a stop, "and you're one of them. Thanks so much."

"My pleasure," he said.

Half an hour later, I was home.

The next morning, Fred inspected the spare inner tube for less than a minute before he recognized it wasn't defective. I hadn't pushed hard enough on the valve to open it.

What a simple solution! Like the time I was locked in the curing room when I was a kid, all I had to do was push harder to get out of trouble. Both times, God could have told me this but didn't. Now I knew: it wasn't because God didn't want to help me out of my darkness, but because I needed to find God in it.

I have spent most of my life trying to get out of dark places like depression, problems, or a myriad of uncomfortable feelings. I always thought that if I could find out how to push open the door and get out, happiness would be just outside. As a result, life became "a series of problems to be solved instead of mysteries to be lived."

I must have heard that pathetically proverbial line a dozen times. But I never understood it until Jesus flicked on the light, and I found God with me in the dark.

18. A DISTURBING SOLUTION TO POVERTY

"IF YOUR CHURCH WANTS to do something about poverty, here's what you should do." Joyce Heron addressed a conference of her peers. This confident pastor lived in Vancouver's Downtown Eastside which has the poorest postal code in Canada. There she ran an outreach ministry called Jacob's Well.

Like the other pastors around me, I had my pen ready to take down every word. She paused and looked us over. "Listen. It's not that complicated. Just find one poor person and be friends with them."

That was it. No programs. No organizing. Find one poor person and love them.

She reminded me of Jean Vanier, founder of L'Arche communities for developmentally disabled people. He claimed loving people who are mentally, physically, emotionally or monetarily poor is the only way to become human. But it's not easy, Vanier says, because poor people are different, and "different people disturb us." [2]

I was willing to be disturbed but didn't know how I was going to find this poor person. Heron read my mind. "Don't worry. You won't have to look very hard to find one. They will find you."

That's for sure. Not long afterwards, I kept running into Cora, a homeless woman in our neighborhood. We chatted

---

[2] Jean Vanier, *Becoming Human.* (Toronto, Ont: House of Anasi Press, 2008), 76.

whenever I saw her, and I gave her food if I had something with me. I'd ask her about her health; she'd ask me about my kids. We promised to pray for each other. I even invited her over to our place for a visit, and one day she took me up on my offer. She left her shopping cart outside our front door and came in for a meal and a good long shower. But still, we're not quite friends.

Other poor people found me too: the morally poor. When I let them into my life, they brought their dispositions with them. In conversations punctuated with profanity, women were objectified, revenge planned, and deceit, promiscuity, and alcoholism normalized. I couldn't ask them to park their inclinations at the door next to Cora's shopping cart. Loving them meant it all came in. But I didn't want it all. And honestly, a part of me was relieved whenever they left.

The poor people I've tried to love disturb me, because they don't stroke my ego or support my worldview. I suspect they are no more comfortable with me than I am with them. Yet Jesus asks me to love them unconditionally.

I used to think that unconditional love meant loving someone who wronged me. I never thought it could mean loving someone who is not so easy to like or doesn't make me feel good. This is too hard, Lord, I prayed.

Jesus didn't say much, but he didn't take the poor people out of my life either. Finally, he pointed me to Julian of Norwich who lived in England in the fourteenth century. She said, "The mark of sovereign friendship of our courteous Lord is that he keeps us so tenderly while we are in sin; and furthermore he touches us so secretly and shows us our sin by the sweet light of mercy and grace."

Julian invited me to take a deep breath and own my poverty. I had to admit I didn't have the resources to love my neighbor, any more than Cora has the resources to house herself.

But we get by. We have both learned to ask for what we need and get used to feeling uncomfortable.

19. WITNESSING GLORY

OUR NEIGHBOR ARRIVED LATE for our new Bible study group. No greeting, no eye contact. He made his confession: he had to buy groceries. Then he hung up his coat and patted his thinning grey hair.

"This is it? No one else is coming?" he asked, seeing only Fred and me.

"They're either sick or have something else going on," I said.

The man sat down, pulled his Bible onto his lap and answered me with scripture, "That's all right. 'For where two or three have gathered together in my name, there I am in their midst,' says the Lord."

"How was your week?" Fred asked him.

"I don't think you want to hear about it." He reminded me of Eeyore in *Winnie the Pooh* as he told us about the irate customer who had phoned him that day at work. "When she found out the washing machine she'd ordered might not be in until next week, she asked to speak to the manager. As if that would help. An hour later the stupid thing arrived, and when I called her back to tell her, she didn't even thank me. And then—" He stopped and shook his head. "No. I won't go on. It'll depress me."

I've heard stories like this from him before. We met at church when our kids were young, and I run into him from time to time on transit. I've seen him waiting for the Skytrain with his lunch box in hand, sitting bent over from the weight of life.

Yet here he was in our living room opening the Book of Hope to Acts 2. We read that the Holy Spirit came like a violent wind and filled the place where the believers met. Tongues of fire rested on each of them. Then they began praising God in different languages, and Peter, the fisherman, boldly preached to the crowd. That day three thousand people repented and were baptized in the name of Jesus.

When we came to the part that said the believers were devoted to one another as well as to the Lord and committed to fellowship, Eeyore had a question. "Is fellowship really necessary?"

"What do you mean?" I asked.

He told us again about the gossip and judgment that had divided his dear brothers and sisters in Christ and destroyed the first church he attended as a young believer. Thirty years later, the sting remained.

"Look at Enoch; he walked with God," he pointed out. "And Elijah and Jesus, they went off into the desert to spend time alone with God. Isn't solitude our higher calling? Doesn't scripture say Christians should be 'set apart'?"

"I don't think we're supposed to be isolated from each other," I replied. "How can we love one another if we don't spend time together?"

"The 'oneness of heart and mind' that the early believers felt for each other, I know about that. I had that once. Maybe it was because I was a new Christian. Maybe it won't ever happen again."

"Maybe God is calling you to it now."

"I . . . I'll have to pray about that." He paused then said, "Last week I felt Christ's presence. It was so powerful; you must have felt it too."

Last week? Was he talking about our Bible study? That evening half a dozen people were there, and we got off on a tangent about prayer. This man hardly said a word. Afterwards he had muttered, "Maybe it's just me, but I don't see why it has to be so complicated." He had sounded disappointed with the discussion. I never would have guessed he had experienced the Holy Spirit so profoundly.

He went on. "My heart suddenly became warm. I felt like the Holy Spirit had wrapped it up in a blanket." He leaned back against the couch. "This happens sometimes when I am alone praying. I was surprised when it happened last week, you know, with people around." We waited for him to go on, but all he said was, "I don't know. Maybe I'm different."

After our neighbor went home, I marveled at the glory we had witnessed. Like a flame at Pentecost the Holy Spirit had come to him in the midst of us, and then as with Peter, gave him the courage to tell us.

20. THE LABYRINTH

I STOOD ON THE deck of the ferry bound for Bowen Island. The city receded; its urgency undone by cloudless blue, circling gulls, and coastal peaks. Two arms of rock and forest that protect Snug Cove welcomed me in.

As I walked up Cates Hill to Rivendell, I wondered what God had in store for me during my first two-day retreat. The wrought iron gate was open, and two deer nibbled salal. If they noticed me walking up the driveway, they kept their observations to themselves. I dropped my backpack off in my room and went to the retreat center's small library to look for a copy of a book I'd forgotten to bring. Sure enough, it was there. But in my search, I found five books on labyrinths.

Unlike a maze, a labyrinth is not a puzzle. There is only one route which leads to the center, then you follow the same way out. For centuries Christians, who wanted to go on a pilgrimage but lacked the time or money, walked labyrinths instead. There must be one here, I thought, and then went off to find a place to pray in the late afternoon sun.

An Adirondack chair that afforded a view of the harbor was unoccupied. I was about to sit down when a voice wafted out of an open window. Then I heard a guitar and people began singing off key. I wandered about, feeling like Goldilocks: nothing was quite right.

Finally I settled for a shaded bench on the north balcony and zipped up my fleece jacket. I closed my eyes and invited Jesus to help me rest in him. Thoughts drifted past, but one image caught my attention: Jesus held my hand and led me down a spiral staircase. The image floated away again, leaving me in peaceful silence.

After a while I felt chilled and renewed my quest for a quiet, sunny spot. Instead I found a signpost. It said "Trail to the Labyrinth" and pointed to a dirt path zigzagging down the embankment. Could this be my spiral staircase?

Through a clearing I looked down and saw a circle fifteen yards across.. My heart leapt. Inside the circle, a stone path with moss and wildflowers along its edges curled back and forth in quarter and half sections around a six-petaled flower at its center. Though this labyrinth had been recently constructed, it seemed ancient, and I longed to join the generations of pilgrims who had walked on similar stones.

A few minutes later, I stood before the labyrinth with a fluttering in my stomach. How do I do this? Where do I go? The path that was well-defined from the viewpoint now seemed obscure. Help me, Holy Spirit. Guide me, I prayed.

I took off my shoes and socks and stepped onto the first cool stone. The path led me in and then to the left, as if I was walking to the tip of a leaf, then back along it to its stem. I travelled along the stem to the edge of the labyrinth's center. A little sob rose into my chest; I crouched down and touched a stone petal. Then the path led me away from the center and out along the labyrinth's rim. My shoulders sagged; my throat ached. But with each step, the Spirit whispered, *I am here, and here, and here.* I realized that even though I was farther in proximity from the center, I was closer to it on my journey.

At first I kept expecting to lose my way, but when the path took me to the left or to the right, I felt reassured. Sometimes I was guided to take only a few steps and then change direction. Other times I was led halfway round the circle. I couldn't easily trace where I'd come from or where I was going. I didn't mind; I walked lightly and listened.

Then, without fanfare, I arrived at the center. Over the next two days, I walked the labyrinth four or five times and was always surprised to find myself there. I sat down on the stamen and lingered at the center of the world.

When I got up to go, I considered ignoring the meandering path and walking straight out. But I couldn't violate the peace in my heart or the intent of those who had laid the stones. I did what thousands of pilgrims have done before me: I re-entered the labyrinth and began my journey home.

As I moved farther and farther from the center, my progress felt anticlimactic. It reminded me that I was getting old. Summer was gone; only autumn and a long winter lay ahead. But the Spirit reassured me that God was not only at the center, but also along the way—*here, and here and here.*

The Lord is near. God is present in the bell, now ringing, calling the community to prayer, in the people on the ferry, in the noisy city streets, and in each step I take down the spiral staircase within.

> *The Lord is near.*
> —Philippians 4:5b

21. A HOME FOR EVERYONE

"A HOME FOR EVERYONE," I said and began to sob.

After I walked the labyrinth, I went back to the lodge at Rivendell to join the others gathered for evening prayers. I sat on the floor with my back against a wall and listened as the leader invited us to reflect on Ecclesiastes 3.

"There is a time for everything," he said. "A time to be born and a time to die; a time to plant and a time to reap; a time to weep and a time to dance. What makes you dance? What gives you joy?"

One person said they were thankful for the beauty of autumn, another for their family, and a third for solitude.

The leader continued. "There is a time to hold on and a time to let go. What is God calling you to let go of?"

People responded, "Disappointment . . . Expectations . . . Wanting people to change."

Then the leader said, "There is a time to plant and a time to reap—a time to harvest hopes that are realized. What hope are you waiting to be realized?"

That's when I heard myself say, "A home for everyone," and a sob awoke in my belly and rose into my throat. If I hadn't caught it, I would have wailed. Instead, trapped in my voice box, it throbbed, and beat against the constriction. I drew my knees to my chin and buried my face in my arms. I couldn't stop crying.

Not until I was alone in my room, did the sob rest. But whenever I think about it, it reawakens. Even now as I write, I can feel it in my throat, this longing for a home for everyone.

A few weeks before I went to Rivendell, I was jogging through a park when I heard a woman yell out, "Come back. Please!" She waved her hand in the air and then doubled over and moaned, "I can't believe this is happening."

I soon learned the woman's name was Carol. She had just cashed her welfare check and came to the park to enjoy a take-out meal along with a fellow she'd met in the welfare line. Before her lunch was over, the man took off with Carol's wallet and the six hundred dollars in it.

I let Carol use my cell phone to speak with a social worker. As the conversation went on and Carol heard that the money wasn't going to be replaced, she grew increasingly distraught. She handed me the phone and began to pace.

"I'm afraid she might harm herself," the social worker said. "Can you stay with her until the police arrive?"

"Sure," I said.

Eventually Carol stopped pacing and lit a cigarette. "He said he was going for a walk. I didn't even see him take my wallet. Why does a person do a thing like that? My roommate's going to beat me when she finds out I have no money."

"Come and sit down," I said calmly. She finished her cigarette and rubbed her fingers over the burn marks on her wrist.

"I thought life would be better now that I'm clean," she said and wrapped her arms around her knees. "I've been raped four times in the last six months."

She pulled a weathered notebook out of her bag and continued, "When I tell people about my life, they shake their heads. They can't believe I'm still alive. They tell me, 'Carol, you could write a book about your life.' So I am. I'm writing it for my sons."

She showed me the pages, dense with blue ink. "One of these chapters is going to be about the day I get my boys back, when we finally have a place of our own."

The police arrived; the officers were soft-spoken and kind.

Carol hugged me goodbye. "Thank you," she said. "I'll never forget you."

I haven't forgotten her either. Though I haven't seen Carol since then, I recognize her in every person I meet. She is a raw version of us all. Every one of us lugs around fear, pain, and vulnerability. People snatch our dreams and leave us pleading for hope. We all long for a home as safe as God's heart, where we can love and care for our own.

22. GIVING BIRTH TO MY FEELINGS

TEARS STREAMED DOWN MY face again as I told my new spiritual director about Rivendell and my stifled sob.

"What made you hold back God's feelings?" she asked.

"That was God?"

"I think so. A few minutes ago you said you might be sensing God's compassion for those who are homeless."

I felt it again, God's holy sob trapped in my throat, rubbing it raw.

"My throat feels tight and sore, as if big feelings want to come out, but the canal's too small."

"Like you're giving birth?"

"Like I'm giving birth to something precious."

The spiritual direction session helped me pay more attention to my feelings. In the days that followed, I noticed that I welcomed hope, confidence, and compassion as affirmations of God's presence. But when I felt irritated, ashamed, or annoyed, God seemed far away. I wondered what I had done wrong.

With some trepidation, I admitted to Jeff Imbach, who was my supervisor at the time, that I felt frustrated and detached while listening to one of my directees. I expected a frown of disapproval, but his face lit up. "Great observation! Why do you think you felt that way?"

"I have no idea."

"Perhaps your directee was getting cold feet. Often when the Holy Spirit draws us closer to God, the intimacy is too much for us, and we try to change course, change the topic—anything to get out of the spotlight. Your feelings alerted you that something like this might be happening to your directee."

"You mean my negative feelings don't always mean I'm doing something wrong?"

"Not at all. Our feelings tell us many things. That's why it's important to listen to them."

Jeff's advice inspired me to summon up my courage and welcome all my feelings—the ones I was grateful for and the ones I wasn't.

Before long I was overwhelmed. "I give up!" I complained to my spiritual director on my next visit. "When I listen to my feelings, I get confused or jump to wrong conclusions. Other times I see more truth than I bargained for. It's too much, too fast."

"Where are you feeling it now in your body?" she asked.

"Here. In my throat." As soon as I said it, I knew what was going on. "I'm in labor."

A tear trickled down my cheek. I was giving birth to something precious to God.

Over time I shared more and more of my feelings with God, even the ones I was ashamed of. I had avoided these because I was afraid of God's reproach. But God has a whole repertoire of responses that doesn't include shaming. When I sat with God in my sadness, we grieved a loss together. When I confessed my anger, the Spirit showed me how it had valiantly defended my boundaries. When I was frustrated, God helped me realign my expectations. When I was overcome with remorse, Jesus held me tenderly and wept.

I am grateful for my feelings, and I pray for the grace to listen to each and every one of them.

23. PATRON SAINT OF THE PERPETUALLY ANNOYED

IT BEGAN INNOCENTLY ENOUGH. All I did was pay attention to my feelings. I noticed I would go along feeling great until someone annoyed me. Then I got angry. What's the matter with them, anyway? Why'd they have to do that? I'd wonder, then plan what I'd say the next time that happened.

On a bike ride, I passed a fellow's house and remembered how he insulted me. On another ride, I recalled someone else I was glad I rarely met. Then there was that woman I worked with twenty years ago. Try as I might, I could not find a way to love her. Sometimes I wished I could put them in a dinghy and push them out to sea where I'd never run into them again. I would even joke that everyone needs one or two people like that in their life. But it wasn't funny anymore; I found an enemy on every street.

I didn't think about them often, and usually if people offended me, I tried to forgive them. But deep in my heart Esther, the Patron Saint of the Perpetually Annoyed, kept a record of their wrongs. For years I ignored her while she quietly pouted in a corner. But one day she had had enough.

That day I got blamed for something that wasn't my fault. My patron saint rose up with righteous indignation and defended me against my offender. A surge of power coursed through my veins.

For days after that she would not be sequestered. She knew she needed to protect me and proved it with a long list of violations. "See, see what they did to you?" she scowled. "I ask you, was that kind?"

Enemies multiplied and surrounded me. Help me! I prayed.

A few days later, I met a part-time hermit at a small gathering of women. The hermit was in her sixties and has a House of Welcome where people come for retreats and spiritual direction. Every day she spends six hours in silence in her hermitage in the garage.

That evening I arrived shrouded in the grey garb of my order. The lady hermit limped in with a cane and a grin. I found out later she had injured her knee dancing.

"I came out of the womb dancing," she said. Every time I glanced at her, she looked at me and loved me.

I sipped Rooibos tea and listened to the conversation. One woman said, "My deepest desire is to love God with my whole being."

"May I offer you some advice?" the hermit asked. "Every morning look at yourself in the mirror and say—with gusto—'Good morning, beloved of God.'"

The next morning I ignored my reflection in the mirror and sat down to pray. I opened my Bible to Psalm 23 and pictured Jesus shepherding my cantankerous saint.

She shook her staff at him and complained, "You say you're my shepherd, but I don't have what I want. Green pastures and quiet waters are not enough. All right, I admit sometimes I feel refreshed, but often I'm frustrated and disappointed. You guide me for a while; then you disappear and leave me stranded. Here I am again in a valley—even darker than the one before—and where are you? Never mind," she said, "I've got my fear and anger to protect me. I know how to sleep with one eye open."

I looked at my fists and saw a cudgel of anger in one hand and a staff of fear in the other. I felt so ashamed, tears streamed down my cheeks.

I closed my eyes, and there was my Shepherd looking at me lovingly, the way the dancing hermit did.

I rested in God's warm gaze until it was time to get ready for my writers' group.

"Good morning, beloved of God," I said with gusto to myself as I put on my make-up.

By the time I arrived at Kyle Center where the group meets, I was as giddy as Scrooge on Christmas Day. Everything was going swimmingly until another writer interrupted me mid-sentence and dismissed my opinion. Disappointment tempted me to retaliate until I saw his clenched fist.

Ah, someone else who sleeps with one eye open, someone else who is beloved of God.

24. SEASONS

"What about my children? Who will look after them?" asked Molly Rush whenever she was asked to join an anti-war demonstration.

I read about Rush one morning in a devotional book. This mother of six and grandmother of two was the director of the Thomas Merton Peace Centre in Pittsburgh. This is why she was often asked to demonstrate. Her response was always the same until one day she asked herself, "What about my children? What will become of them if we continue to build weapons of destruction?"

The story was written to inspire me to follow Rush's example and become more actively involved in peacemaking. Groan. One more thing to add to my "A Good Christian Should" list.

Many Christians keep such lists. They are rarely in a notebook or taped to the fridge. Instead we record these expectations on virtual Post-it notes and stick them onto ourselves, so we won't forget them. "I Should Protest" was already on my left shoulder between "Exercise more" and "Care for the widows and orphans." This unconscious habit of "should" collecting, begun with youthful idealism, has given my guilt a thousand places to land.

The weight of my list wearied me until one day I realized I didn't need it. God knows what I should be doing and when. So, after reading the devotional, instead of assuming I should follow Molly Rush's example, I thought for a moment.

It's not wrong to ignore a worthy cause to look after our children. Many neglected children of workaholic parents can attest to that. Nor is it wrong to leave our children for a while in order to fight injustice. Perhaps for a season, God wanted Molly to tend to her children, and in another she was called to protest. She could even take her children with her. The question is not "What should a good Christian do?" but "God, what do you want me to do right now, in this season?"

A timely question. Not long after my encounter with Carol in the park, Wanda Mulholland from the Burnaby Task Force on Homelessness gave a presentation at our church. A month later, seventeen people who had heard her speak were eager to do something to end homelessness. But between Wanda's presentation and the follow-up meeting, life took an unexpected turn. A cruel winter set in, and I needed to be with my family as much as possible to cook meals, hold the baby, and listen, listen, listen.

A good pastor should be on the forefront leading the way, but I had to confess to these seventeen people that I couldn't give them any extra time or energy.

"We understand," said a volunteer, who then offered to organize an outreach event without my help.

What a relief. I didn't have to do it all. God knows we can't plant in the winter and harvest in the spring without fighting the flow of the universe. Solomon asked, "What does a worker gain from their toil?" Indeed, what is to be gained by trying to force a spade into frozen ground?

We do not serve a one-size-fits-all God with an unyielding "to do" list. God knows us, loves us, and makes everything beautiful in its time.

25. IN MARTHA'S DEFENSE

As Jesus and his disciples were on their way, he came to a village where a woman named Martha opened her home to him. She had a sister called Mary, who sat at the Lord's feet listening to what he said. But Martha was distracted by all the preparations that had to be made. She came to him and asked, "Lord, don't you care that my sister has left me to do the work by myself? Tell her to help me!"

"Martha, Martha," the Lord answered, "you are worried and upset about many things, but few things are needed—or indeed only one. Mary has chosen what is better, and it will not be taken away from her."

—Luke 10:38-42

MOST WOMEN I KNOW don't find the story of Mary and Martha comforting. Jesus reprimands Martha, the busy bee, because she doesn't follow Mary's example and sit down. What's up with that? If everyone was a Mary, we'd starve to death.

Shouldn't Jesus praise Martha for being like Paul who told us to run the good race, or like Jesus himself who laid down his life for his friends? On the other hand, what would have happened if Jesus had praised Martha for her acts of service? Imagine Jesus smiling at Martha and saying, "You go, girl!" Martha would be up the next morning, alarm set for five and hearing the voice of Jesus say, "Imagine what you could do if you got up at 4:45?" How messed up is that?

Equally messed up is making a saint out of the laid-back introvert. We often assume that Mary is more attentive to Jesus because of her temperament. However, a process-oriented introvert can be as distracted as a goal-oriented extrovert. I know people who have no trouble relaxing, but thoughts of Jesus don't enter their heads. Instead of busying themselves with work, they preoccupy themselves with ideas, sleep, or amusements.

Jesus loved Martha. It was out of kindness that he told her the best thing she could do was sit down and be with him.

This got me wondering: can church become a safe place for Martha? I am both a spiritual director and a pastor. One day I applaud the Martha who doesn't take on another job because she is heeding an inner call to be still, and the next I try to find ten people to work in the kitchen for a church event. If everyone rests, who will care for those who are sick or homeless? Who will teach Sunday school or serve coffee after Sunday worship?

Questions like these make us do things out of guilt, and that guilt fuels Christians already steeped in the Protestant work ethic. The act of being busy for the Lord is praised by church leaders with gift certificates and accolades. Churches regularly exploit Christians who want to burn out for Jesus.

Unfortunately these Marthas do that. They burn out and end up—you guessed it—at the feet of Jesus, where they feel disoriented, disappointed, resentful, and empty. They confess, "I don't know who I am anymore." They cry, "Lord, have mercy." And years later these redeemed Marthas will tell you, it was the best thing that ever happened to them.

What if we simply did what Jesus said? What if we did the "one thing needed"—interrupted our work, sat down for a minute, and listened to Jesus? Maybe we wouldn't be so quick to grab our aprons and start chopping vegetables. Maybe we would find space to discern whether our actions come from attending to our fears or responding to God's love.

At Jesus' feet we learn when and how to work. Jesus helps us filter through the guilt-ridden demands around and within us, so we can recognize God's voice.

The more I rest with Jesus, the more I discover how considerate and thoughtful he is. Sometimes his only job for me is to enjoy the beauty of a tree, to feel how much he cherishes me, or to notice a little miracle. Like what happened one Sunday not long ago.

That day a baby boy was being baptized. Before church started, his grandmother was looking for a glass pickle dish she'd left behind at a congregational lunch the week before. She couldn't find it anywhere. When it came time for the baptism, the family went forward. Scripture was read and vows said. Then our pastor dipped his hand in a little bowl of water to bless and baptize the infant. At that moment the grandmother realized the bowl he was using was her pickle dish. Can you imagine her joy when she saw it used for such a glorious purpose? God thinks of everything. I can relax at the feet of a Lord like that.

I figure the best gift we can give Martha is space—space to say no and just be, space to get tired of avoiding God, and space to hear where the true desires of her heart line up with God's plans for heaven on earth.

Let's give Martha a break. We can trust that, in time, God will inspire a redeemed Martha to want to wash dishes for the glory of God. Jesus knew exactly what he was doing when he simplified life down to one thing. What kind of church would we be if we trusted him enough to do it?

26. ON THE EIGHTH DAY GOD PAINTED MY OFFICE

"This is your office? It looks more like a storage room. Do you actually work here?" my friend asked.

"Well, no. But now that my hours have been increased to twenty a week, I'm supposed to."

"Any money in the church budget to spruce it up a little? No, eh? See this wallpaper; it's got to be thirty years old. You know, a good coat of paint would do wonders."

Creating beautiful spaces doesn't come naturally to me, although it was on my mind. Our church had recently voted to raise money to beautify our windowless, boxlike sanctuary. Artists that attend New Life advocated for this change. Beauty—in nature, art, and architecture—inspires them to worship God. But for me, beauty has always been an afterthought, an impractical extravagance. Besides, my world disappears when I close my eyes to pray or turn on the computer to write. I could happily worship or work in a plain old box.

"I wouldn't know where to begin," I said.

"I'll help you. It won't take much more than a day to do these two walls anyway. The third wall could be an accent shade and—"

She inspected the floor to ceiling bookshelves crammed with ice cream buckets, tablecloths, communion supplies, and old photo albums. "Is there anywhere else you can put this stuff?"

The next week I found new homes for the clutter on the shelves, the soup ministry's canopy and the orange metal desk I had inherited.

I told my hairdresser who is one of the New Life artists, that I was thinking of painting my office. She stopped snipping and beamed at me in the mirror. "I've got the most gorgeous paint for you. I've been saving it for something like this."

I went home with two gallons of sage-colored paint and primer. I felt like God and these two women were already rolling up their sleeves and getting out the brushes. I wanted to join them, but my life was already packed to the edges. When did I have time to paint? Then I remembered that my friend had said it would only take a day. Wasn't that what she said?

Next Tuesday Fred made sure I had the equipment I needed and added a few essentials he said I couldn't do without. Wednesday morning my friend arrived at the church ready to paint.

"This is exciting," she said, "but I have to warn you. Your office will be so beautiful, everyone's going to want to use it." I liked that prospect.

She glanced over the supplies and set aside a few of Fred's "essentials." I brushed off my anxiety and began sponging water onto the wall and stripping off the ancient paper. After lunch we puttied holes. While waiting for the filler to dry, we searched around the church for better furniture. We found spare lamps in the prayer room and two comfy armchairs and a coffee table that were taking up space in a Sunday school room. She knew what colors went together well, and when she held the paint lid against each piece of furniture, I agreed with her choices.

"I don't think we need the primer," she said after we sanded and wiped down the walls. She stuck a brush into the paint and slathered some on the accent wall—the wall I was leaving for later. "What do you think? Do you like it? If not, we can get another color."

I didn't answer her right away; I was wrapping my mind around the fact that I was now committed to paint that wall.

"You need to be sure you like it," she persisted.

"Yes, I do," I replied, relieved that I actually did.

"All right, now let's see if it goes with the bookshelves." She dabbed more paint on the fourth wall. My heart sank again. No choice now about painting that wall either. "Yup," she said and stood back to see if the paint matched the wood. "This'll be fine."

Once we got painting and continued the morning's conversation, I forgot about the time and began to enjoy myself.

At four-thirty she called it a day.

"Oh, darlin'," she said, reading the disappointment on my face. "The second coat won't take long." She touched the swatch of sage on the unpainted wall. "Sorry. I got a little carried away."

"Never mind, I really like how it's turning out."

On Thursday I was at home reading Bible commentaries to prepare for an upcoming sermon. But when I found myself rereading the same line a third time, I decided to go and paint.

"Let me help you," said a man from our church after he watched me for a minute or two. "I used to paint houses for a living." He showed me the "right way" to hold a brush and rolled paint liberally over the surfaces.

"Do you think I'll have enough paint to finish the room?" I asked.

"Oh sure," he replied, confidently. I bit my lip and hoped it was true.

Friday evening Fred and I dismantled the bookshelves so that we could finish painting the next day. When he saw his unused supplies and the full can of primer, he gave me a quizzical look.

I threw up my hands. "Everyone's an expert!" Rather than join the ranks of everyone, he said nothing more.

Saturday morning Fred and I primed the third and fourth walls, hoping we'd have enough paint to finish the job. Meanwhile my friend dropped by with two paintings—an abstract and a Monet.

That afternoon I breathed a sigh of relief. Every last drop of paint was gone, but finally we were done. The walls were warm and inviting.

We returned that evening to put the shelves back together, and discovered I had missed a few spots. That night I lay awake.

"Do you think we can buy more paint?" I asked Fred who was trying to sleep.

"You'd never get a good enough match. Besides, it's not that bad."

"Maybe not for you, but it bothers me."

Sunday morning as soon as it was a reasonable hour, I called my hairdresser friend. "Do you have any more paint left?"

"I'll have to see," she said, unable to mask her doubt.

But she arrived for church, triumphantly carrying a can of paint in each hand.

A few weeks later, I walked into my office to discover two kids sitting in the comfy chairs. "Is this your office?" one asked. "It's beautiful."

Once again the room's warmth enfolded me. I looked at the soft sage-colored walls and remembered how much work they'd been. When we ran out of paint, I felt as if I had been banished from Eden after only a glimpse. But when more paint was found, I understood how much God loves beauty and wants to share it.

It seems obvious now that the One who created orchids, butterflies, and waterfalls would like to be worshipped in a beautiful sanctuary. I had thought God was like me and had more important things to do than sit around painting daisies. Now I know God has time for it all.

27. PEACE, BE STILL

MARK'S GOSPEL SAYS THAT one evening Jesus got into a boat with his disciples to cross the Sea of Galilee. He was exhausted after a day of teaching and healing and fell asleep on a cushion at the back of the boat. A while later a fierce squall threatened to swamp them. The disciples woke Jesus. "Teacher, don't you care if we drown?"

Unperturbed Jesus stood up and addressed the elements. "Peace! Be still!" The wind died down and the sea calmed.

I picture the disciples sitting in that boat, hands clenched to the railing as the rolling seas begin to settle. I can hear the last few waves lap against the boat's hull until finally there is no sound at all. I can see the disciples, surrounded by stillness, rising in awe.

When I was in college, I swam twice a week at the YWCA. One morning I was the first one there. I rushed onto the pool deck, goggles in hand, to do my lengths, but the sight of the pool without one ripple in it stopped me. I had never seen the water this still before. I was reluctant to dive in and disturb it. What would it be like to embody such stillness?

I am rarely still. Even when I sit down to pray, my mind doesn't stop whirring. I shut my eyes—as if this were a switch that makes me instantly present to God—and, without wasting a minute, I shout over the din of the waves and strain to hear Christ's voice in the tumult.

But when I read this story again, Jesus whispers to my busy mind, *Peace! Be still.*

It takes time to become still. There is no way to hasten the process; Jesus knows that. But eventually my soul quiets down.

What does God do in this stillness? Who knows? For when I am finally at peace, I entertain neither thought nor feeling, so I have nothing to report. But when I think about it afterwards, I notice a delightful warmth residing in my chest. In the days that follow, I discover new freedoms.

I can imagine that as I waited for the waves to settle, the Holy Spirit hovered closer and closer then finally came to rest on the still surface of my soul.

> *Calm the waves of this heart, O God;*
> *calm its tempests.*
> *Calm yourself, O my soul,*
> *so that God is able to rest in you,*
> *so that God's peace may cover you.*
> *Yes, you give us peace, O God,*
> *peace that the whole world can never take away.*
> —Soren Kierkegaard (1813–1855)

28. THE GIRL BY THE DOOR

ONE MORNING I WONDERED why it's difficult for me to sit still and be with God. Then a memory from my preteen years came to mind.

I was passing through the kitchen on the way to my bedroom when my mom said, "Wait a minute."

She closed the hall door, then the dining room door. I hugged my school books and bit my lip. My mom rarely raised her voice, never her hand, but when she lifted up her forefinger as she was doing then, I knew I was in trouble.

"I have a bone to pick with you," she said.

She had found out that I read my sister's diary and revealed a secret to my friends. When my sister, who is two years older than me, got teased about having a crush on a certain boy, she put two and two together.

Of course what I did was wrong, and I should have been corrected. But I don't remember that part. All I remember is the doors closing, the finger raised like a judge's gavel, and any proof of my goodness flitting away like butterflies.

Even now, nearly forty years later, that little girl is still inside me. She reluctantly comes to pray. I often see her in my mind; arms crossed, she stands by the door waiting for the time to pass. No matter how sweet or loving my Lord is, she keeps waiting for God to raise a finger and say, "I have a bone to pick with you."

"How can I be sure God isn't going to get mad at me?" this little girl asks. "Jesus had plenty of bones to pick with the

Pharisees, his disciples, and his mother. He even had something unpleasant to say to that Samaritan woman."

A week later "that Samaritan woman" came up in conversation. "You know the story of the woman at the well," my co-worker said, "when Jesus told her she had been married five times, and the man she was living with wasn't her husband? It never occurred to me until now that her reaction says volumes. She didn't go out and tell people, 'Hey watch out! There's a guy by the well who knows all the dirt on you.' She said, 'Come and see a man who knows everything I ever did.' I think something happened when she was with Jesus. He must have let her know—maybe in his eyes or in the tone of his voice—that he loved her, no matter what she had done."

The next morning as I began to pray, I invited the hurt little girl in me to think about what my co-worker had said. I imagined Jesus meeting the Samaritan woman at the well. He comes along, tired from his journey, and asks her for a drink of water. She stands holding her bucket; he sits looking up at her. He offers to quench her perpetual thirst with living water, but not before they talk for a while about their religious differences, the coming Messiah, and her infidelities.

How would Jesus speak to me about my infidelity? He might be less interested in what I did, than why I did it. Why did I read my sister's diary? Was it a lark, or did I hope to find my name written in it? Did I long for evidence that she saw something good in me? Do I thirst for the same from Jesus?

Oh, yes. I'll take this water you offer, Lord, I prayed and hoped it would satisfy my wary little self. But in the days that followed, I didn't find it any easier to pray. The little girl still waited by the door.

Not long afterwards I thought of another way to convince her to pray. In my imagination I took her hand, and we sat down together. Then I taught her how to center herself in God. We closed our eyes and let our thoughts drift by. I felt peaceful for a while then, without realizing it, I began planning what to make for supper.

I felt a gentle tug on my arm. "Come back and pray," the little girl whispered. "God is all I ever hoped for." She paused and closed her eyes again, then added, "No. More."

I thought her story was over, but a few days later I was reading Psalm 84, and these words caught my attention, "I'd rather be a doorkeeper in the house of my God than dwell…" I closed my eyes and saw my little doorkeeper.

The Holy Spirit seemed to say, *Let her be there as long as she wants. At least she's inside the door.*

29. STRETCHING MORE THAN THE HEAVENS

Do you not know?
  Have you not heard?
Has it not been told you from the beginning?
  Have you not understood since the earth was founded?
He sits enthroned above the circle of the earth,
  and its people are like grasshoppers.
He stretches out the heavens like a canopy,
  and spreads them out like a tent to live in.
He brings princes to naught
  and reduces the rulers of this world to nothing.
No sooner are they planted,
  no sooner are they sown,
  no sooner do they take root in the ground,
than he blows on them and they wither,
  and a whirlwind sweeps them away like chaff.
"To whom will you compare me?
  Or who is my equal?" says the Holy One.
Lift up your eyes and look to the heavens:
  Who created all these?
He who brings out the starry host one by one
  and calls forth each of them by name.
Because of his great power and mighty strength,
  not one of them is missing.
Why do you complain, Jacob?
  Why do you say, Israel,

> "My way is hidden from the LORD;
> my cause is disregarded by my God"?
> Do you not know?
> Have you not heard?
> The LORD is the everlasting God,
> the Creator of the ends of the earth.
> He will not grow tired or weary,
> and his understanding no one can fathom.
> He gives strength to the weary
> and increases the power of the weak.
> Even youths grow tired and weary,
> and young men stumble and fall;
> but those who hope in the LORD
> will renew their strength.
> They will soar on wings like eagles;
> they will run and not grow weary,
> they will walk and not be faint.
> —Isaiah 40:21-31

WHY MEMORIZE SCRIPTURE? It's a lot of work, and I have enough of that to do. But one Sunday the children's pastor stood before our congregation and held up a piece of paper with a bunch of letters on it. She assured us that this teaching tool would make it easier to memorize Isaiah 40:21-31. The skeleton had the first letter of every word in the Bible passage listed line by line. I was curious, so I gave it a try.

She was right. Soon I was able to recite the twelve verses using only the skeleton. Weeks later I knew the passage by heart. As I meditated on it, Isaiah asked me, "Do you not know? Have you not heard? Has it not been told you from the beginning? Have you not understood since the earth was founded?" And I was caught again—acting as if God doesn't exist. Isaiah's questions took the wind out of my anxiety and anchored me in the reality that God is always present.

Isaiah also said that God "sits enthroned above the circle of the earth . . . and spreads out the heavens like a tent to live in." Instantly I recalled Heidi at seven years of age. With a bit of string and a bright pink sarong, she made herself a tent. When she emerged from her canopy like a princess, we addressed her as the "Memsahib." I see the same playfulness in our Creator. According to Isaiah, God brings out the stars one by one and calls them each by name. Just like Heidi lined up her stuffed animals, God made sure "not one of them was missing."

Isaiah's poetry led me to revel in God's majesty, productivity, imagination, justice, and compassion. God is incomparably perceptive, everlasting, inexhaustible, understanding, kind, empowering, trustworthy and strong.

"Did you know that 'weak' or 'weary' is used five times in this passage?" I told the children's pastor as we set up tables for Sunday school. When I looked more closely, I counted twenty-nine references to weakness in these verses. Isaiah claimed that God creates and alleviates weakness, reducing rival powers to chaff and renewing the hopeful weary with strength. As I walked around with Isaiah 40 on my lips, I enjoyed the fact that God knows I am weak and will strengthen me.

But on the Sunday I was scheduled to preach and woke up with a weakness called laryngitis, I was not amused. Where was the strength God promised? No matter how hard I tried, I couldn't get my voice to rise above a squeaky whisper. Thankfully, the youth pastor was able to fill in for me.

I put my sermon notes away and sighed. *Why are you doing this, God?* And the words of Isaiah came to me: "Why do you say, Esther, 'My way is hidden from the LORD; my cause is disregarded by my God'? Do you not know? Have you not heard?"

No one can fathom God's understanding. Something good would come of this, Isaiah led me to believe.

The next day, Fred and I took Heidi—now grown—and her new baby to visit my parents in the Okanagan. I could hardly speak. I accepted this unwelcome vow of silence for the sole reason that if my voice improved I might be able to preach the next Sunday. I rationed my words, hoarding them like my first allowance.

The enforced silence stretched me. I began to notice how often I wanted to correct or criticize (ouch!). I also noticed I didn't like the long pauses in conversations or the fact that I had to spend precious words prompting Fred to speak up (my parents are somewhat deaf). Without words, it was difficult to be understood or appreciated by anyone except my little grandson.

I read a lot, but that nearly did me in. My book was full of new concepts, and it was hard to digest them alone. I sucked throat lozenges, gargled with salt water, and wished I had an antacid for my brain. The silence stretched me so thin my weaknesses showed through.

But empowering weakness is God's specialty. Isaiah says if we hope in the Lord, God will renew our strength, and we will rise on wings like eagles. The next Sunday, I did rise with more strength in my voice than I had the week before and was able to preach. However the sermon I gave was humbler than the one I had originally prepared.

I used to question why anyone would bother memorizing scripture. But now I know. If I had only read Isaiah 40, I would never have set up my tent, gazed at the heavens, and thanked God for stretching me.

30. TRAIN WRECK

Love the Lord your God with all your heart and with all your soul and with all your mind and with all your strength . . .[and] love your neighbor as yourself. —*Mark 12:30, 31*

I WAS READING THESE verses in Mark when the phone rang. It was the young mother who used to live next door.

"I know this is short notice, but could you look after Jordie for a couple of hours?"

I looked outside. The clouds had disappeared and blue sky beckoned me. Lord, I prayed, do you mean this neighbor? Now?

"Today's not good," I said, "but next week—"

"A unit's come available in the housing complex up the hill. If I don't take it, I'll have to wait a long time for another. I'd ask my mother to babysit, but she got called in to work."

I checked the time. I had planned to go for a bike ride, but that wasn't the only complication. The woman's husband lived in the townhouse next to ours. He worked an early shift and usually arrived home at noon. Since the two of them had separated, he bristled like a cat whenever she was around.

"When will you be back?"

"Oh, eleven, at the latest. The ministry worker said she would meet me at nine-thirty. Thanks, Esther," she said and hung up.

When the young mom returned around eleven-thirty, Jordie and I were outside playing. He threw up his hands with glee when he saw his mother, but she didn't notice.

"She just had a three bedroom unit to show me," she ranted. "I already told her I could barely afford a two bedroom one."

"Is that it?"

"I'm afraid so," she said. "But I kind of liked the place. It has a cute little backyard. My cousin from the Island wants to move to the city. He could help pay the rent."

"You mean the guy that stayed with you last summer? Isn't he the one who kept borrowing money and never helped with the housework?"

"He was going through a tough time, and I can't keep living with my mom. Jordie gets on her nerves." On cue the toddler squealed and ran after a dog. I managed to scoop him up before he got to the street. He curled his arms around my neck and kissed me. His mother smiled.

"I'd be flattered," I said, "but he seems to be kissing everything—the teeter totter, the slide. . ."

"Da-da!" The child nearly leapt out of my arms.

"Hey, buddy. Come to see me for a while?" My neighbor dropped his backpack on the ground, and held out his arms.

"We have to go," his wife said.

"I've got the whole afternoon free. I'll bet Jordie would love to go down and throw stones in the creek with me. Wouldn't you, buddy?"

"Don't start with me. He needs a nap."

The man straightened his back and moved toward us. "I have a right to see my own son."

"Don't," I said softly.

"I'm taking him home." The woman reached out to take her child.

"No, you're not." The angry man shoved his wife out of the way. She fell to the pavement and landed on her hip, arm, then cheek.

He backed away, snatched up his pack and was heading toward the bus stop by the time his wife was on her feet again. "That's assault, you know? I'm calling the cops," she yelled.

She grabbed Jordie and cuddled him. "I'm sorry," she mumbled. A tear slid down her grazed cheek, and her arm began to bleed. The toddler was strangely silent.

By the time I'd washed and bandaged her arm, the police arrived. She gave her statement to the officer while I got Jordie something to eat.

I was peeling him a banana when the police officer poked her head into the kitchen. "Did you see what happened?" she asked.

I steadied my trembling hands on the counter. "It was like watching a train wreck."

An hour later I was alone again. I got into my biking clothes and headed out. The sky was as blue as ever. How could it pretend nothing happened?

31. BEING HERE

"I CAN'T BELIEVE WE'RE here," I sighed as we crested Richter Pass and drove into the arid little town of Osoyoos.

On previous visits we cycled up and down this valley of manicured vineyards, cherry orchards, fruit stands, and tents where the French Canadian backpacking, dread-locked fruit pickers lived. Streets named Gala, Spartan, and other apple varieties house mostly retirees who sell things like used toilets or scooters on their front lawns. Along the lake shore are upscale condos where seasonal residents can easily walk to the Windmill and choose from forty-eight flavors of ice cream. The local hardware store stocks everything from gardening supplies to fair trade coffee. Behind Main Street you'll often see Earl and his black lab, Quincy, with their shopping cart full of cast-offs and tied-on treasures.

We've been coming to Osoyoos once or twice a year since my sister-in-law inherited the condominium from her parents. Their portraits greeted us as we entered the home where they once entertained children and grandchildren, played with their dachshunds, and identified every bird that flew over the lake. Arthur's binoculars were still on the kitchen counter, ready for the meadowlarks' return.

Within an hour of arriving, Fred uncorked the Pinot Noir, and we eased our bodies into the over-sized tub.

"I can't believe we're here," I said again.

The next morning I brewed a cup of fair trade coffee and sat down in the living room to pray. Everything was as I remembered it except for the arrangement of figurines on the mantelpiece. The familiar bronze statue of a mother quail and her two chicks and a collection of tiny people carved out of wood had been moved aside to make space for a nativity scene. Mary, Joseph, two shepherds, and an angel stood around Jesus in swaddling clothes lying in a manger.

No one's been here since Christmas, I thought as I got up for a closer look. The Bethlehem group was deep in contemplation. Meanwhile the quails were itching to go somewhere. At the other end of the mantelpiece, a septuagenarian couple, hands in pockets, viewed the Messiah from afar with a "Golly!" on their lips. A granny waited in her rocking chair, hands folded on her lap, and a stocky Swiss Appenzeller with britches and a wide brimmed hat laughed from his belly.

They were too far from the manger. The Appenzeller was about to burst, so I chose him first and put him beside Mary where he could get a good look at the baby. Then I placed the old couple next to Joseph and sat the granny in front of them. I beheld the new tableau, and joy tickled my chest.

There was room for more. The quails dwarfed the growing family, but I moved them in anyway and felt St. Francis' blessing as I did.

More. On the bureau next to the fireplace was a whole shelf of clay dachshunds. I found one the right size and put him in front of the manger where he could sniff the Holy Child.

There's room for all in Christ's loving gaze: retirees, shop owners, fruit pickers, Earl, Quincy, and Fred and me too. Just as this home longed for its family to return, so does our Lord.

32. HEADWINDS

OUR TEN-DAY OSOYOOS vacation began well. For the first few days, I enjoyed plenty of time to bike, read, and unwind. But I woke up on the fourth day feeling blue for no apparent reason.

The day was cloudy and cool when we parked the car at Vaseau Lake Provincial Park. Without much conversation, Fred and I cycled north through rolling hills along the east side of Skaha Lake and beside the canal to Penticton, where we had arranged to have lunch with old friends.

We got off our bikes, and I looked at my odometer. Had it really taken less than ninety minutes? I must be in pretty good shape, I thought until Fred said, "That was some tailwind! It must be blowing twenty or thirty knots."

I sighed. An infinite number of whitecaps on Okanagan Lake confirmed his observation. My fitness level had not improved, and this tailwind meant the return ride of another twenty miles would be a chore, unless the wind shifted in our favor.

But in the afternoon, the wind was even stronger than it had been earlier. The safer route back, now that people would be heading home from work, was on the main road, which had wide shoulders but higher hills. The two-hour return ride was grueling and noisy.

The following day a new washer and dryer were delivered and installed in the condo. After Fred ran a load of washing and was convinced the machine had been installed properly, we went for a walk. An hour later we returned to find a brightly colored note taped to the front door. While we were out, water had leaked from the laundry room into the suite below, and the on-site manager had shut it off at the source. My sister-in-law, who owned the condo, called from Calgary wondering what was going on. In the end, the damage to both suites was minimal. But a water restoration company needed to be called. They brought a huge noisy blower that was to be left on as much as possible. So much for solitude.

That evening our friends Jack and Valerie arrived from Vancouver to spend the weekend with us. I hoped their company would lift my mood. As Fred put the finishing touches on his curry dinner, we relaxed on the balcony. Jack opened a bottle of Chardonnay, Valerie's favorite.

They were glad to get away. A number of difficulties with work and family had them on their knees in prayer.

"But we're doing, all right," Valerie said. "We can't do anything about it anyway. We have no choice but to trust God."

And she did. Valerie was tired, for sure, yet an inner peace carried her like a tailwind. Meanwhile a little water problem and a noisy blower unnerved me. Any stray comment made me anxious. I wanted to hibernate.

The next morning we gave Valerie some time to herself while the guys and I biked to Oliver and back.

All I have to do is be here in this moment, I thought looking up at the cloudless sky. Fred and Jack dawdled behind, discussing interesting inventions and scientific theories. I ignored them and turned on my iPod. The band, Mutemath, sang over and over, "You are mine, you are mine" as I glided along the smooth winding road, past bush after bush of blossoming lilacs. With a fresh surge of energy, I powered up the hill to the Quinta Ferreira winery.

While I waited for the guys to catch up, I drank in the magnificent view of McIntyre Bluff, the little town of Oliver, and the surrounding lakes and hills. *You are mine. You are mine.*

Jack arrived first, puffing but elated that he didn't have to get off his bike and push it up the hill. Impulsively I told him what I experienced, "It was as if Jesus himself was telling me I was his." A sudden joy made me tear up.

I could see Jack was moved too. He cleared his throat and mumbled something about that being nice and went off to see if the winery was open.

Inside the tasting room, there were more delicious moments: displays of art and award-winning Chardonnay.

"We'll be back with Valerie," we promised.

I hoped that my encounter with God would cause a wind shift in my soul. But later that day the headwinds picked up again.

33. ASTRONOMICAL UNITS

Saturday I awoke feeling indifferent to the May sunshine. My mood didn't improve when I remembered we planned to go to the Dominion Observatory with our friends, Valerie and Jack, who were staying with us in Osoyoos for a few days.

After breakfast we got into our friends' blue Honda and headed north. On the way we passed a fruit stand with a red and white CLOSED sign on the window. I imagined the owner safely at home reading a paperback and sipping coffee.

That's me: CLOSED. I've had enough truth for one season, thank you very much. I don't want to witness any more train wrecks or hear any more bad news from the TV, the mirror, or my bathroom scales. I need no more evidence of how messed up we are or how little I have to show for my life. I know "the truth shall set you free," but that's assuming you survive the shock of hearing it first. Solomon, in his wisdom, should have added another verse to Ecclesiastes 3: "There is a season to be open and a season to be closed." I was certainly closed for the season.

White Lake Road led us into the vacant hills above Oliver to the Dominion Radio Astrophysical Observatory, the only one of its kind in Canada. A sign instructed us to park outside the gate and walk in. Motor vehicles interfered with the reception of radio waves emitted from the hydrogen gases in outer space. I learned this from a disembodied voice after pushing the green button for English.

We walked past rows and rows of telephone poles strung with wires once used to receive radio waves. At the end of the long deserted driveway was a model of the solar system painted on the pavement. Of course the guys had to read every bit of information next to each planet. I consoled myself with the thought that maybe there was nothing more to see when a man walked by.

"Would you like a tour?" he asked, and like faithful hounds, Fred and Jack followed him into the visitors' center.

Wendell Shuster introduced himself then explained how radio waves are used to map portions of the sky. When Jack supplied the scientific terms Wendell was trying politely to avoid and Fred nodded, Wendell rubbed his chin with glee.

After giving complete explanations of the exhibits, Wendell led us up to the control room where we got a closer look at the telescope. "Astronomers around the world take turns operating the radio telescope and share the data they collect," he said. Then he calculated on a blackboard how much time we have left before the sun burns up. Just as I thought: it wasn't going to interrupt our wine tasting that afternoon.

Finally Wendell took us back outside and stood on the pavement between Saturn and Mars.

"I want you to hold your pinkie finger up to the sky like this," he said. "Do you know what's behind the piece of sky it blocks?"

"Thousands of stars?" Valerie guessed.

"Thousands of *galaxies*. At least five thousand of them."

"Huh!" she said. Wendell grinned and asked if we knew what an astronomical unit was.

"The distance from the earth to the sun," Fred answered.

"Right. Now using the scale of the model we're standing on, in which one astronomical unit is a foot, how far do you think it would be to the nearest star?"

"From here to Kamloops," Jack said, admitting he had read it on an exhibit inside.

"Right again," Wendell said. "That's about one hundred and fifty miles away. So, one hundred and fifty times the number of feet in a mile—that's 5,280—times the distance from here to the sun: that's how far it is to the nearest star."

"Wow!" we said in unison, and Wendell was pleased.

Sunday morning instead of going to church, we decided to have our own time of worship. Valerie put on a CD, and we sang along, praising "the God of wonders beyond our galaxy." She had chosen Psalm 103 as our theme, and I volunteered to lead us through the scripture by asking a few basic questions. Even though my mood hadn't lifted, I figured I could do that.

Fred read a portion of the psalm aloud. After a few minutes of silence, I said, "This time as Jack reads the psalm again, listen for a word or phrase that speaks to you."

I closed my eyes and heard, "For as high as the heavens are above the earth, so great is his love for those who fear him." Wonder shot through me.

Thanks to Wendell Shuster, I could now measure in astronomical units the enormity of God's love.

This love reverberated inside and around me. I imagined it whirling up into space and tingling the telephone wires of the Dominion Observatory. I watched it flow to generation after generation, out into the cosmos and back again. And when it returned to me, I threw open every window in my soul to receive it.

34. ENOUGH COMPASSION

"HE WHO DIES WITH the most toys wins," boasts a bumper sticker. Yes *he*. Most women don't think like that. What would bumper sticker philosophy say about us? Perhaps, "she who dies with the most friends wins."

That makes me envision my own funeral. For a few hours, I'll be the center of attention while people tell each other what I did or said that touched them. Sometimes I regret that I won't be there to enjoy it. Other times I'm glad I'll be dead-deaf, especially when I remember the birthday party I had one year when only three guests showed up.

I have to admit that I envy my friend, June. Everyone loves her, including me. June personifies compassion. She always asks how I'm doing, and she really wants to know. When life is good, she wants to hear all about it, and when it isn't, I see tears in her eyes. She never parts without giving me a hug.

Meanwhile I pray, Teach me how to love like that. I wish I was less self-centered.

Yesterday I got together with June and four other women from church. We meet monthly to listen to what's going on in our lives and pray together. June has been on stress leave from her work as a nurse practitioner. We were anxious to hear about her recent meeting with the occupational psychiatrist who assessed her ability to return to work.

"He spent two hours with me. Two hours—asking questions about everything: my family, my work environment, my childhood. Then he said I was in the top five percent of the population born with an acute sensitivity to the feelings and needs of others. However when he took into account my family history and how often I cared for my mother instead of playing like the rest of my peers, he put me in the top one percent of caregivers."

She continued, "He said I'm the type of person everyone wants to hire. Patients, co-workers, and bosses love people like me. It's because we're always there for them. The problem, the psychiatrist said, is that women like me don't know how to care for themselves. Goodness! Who has time for that when there are so many other people to think about? By the time we turn forty we're done. Though we are the best at what we do, eventually our own giftedness does us in. He told me I might not be able to return to this type of work."

"You're kidding," I said.

"I know. I was shocked," June said. "I asked him who could do this kind of work. Who does survive? And he said the large percentage of mediocre caregivers. They are able to be present with others when they are with them and not be concerned about them when they're not."

I listened to my friends' reactions. They too are compassionate, self-sacrificing caregivers. Each one confessed that they carried a heavy load and could relate to this woman's experience. Then all five looked at me.

"How do you do it?" one asked. "You have quite a bit on your plate, being a pastor and all. How do you keep from going under?"

"Oh," I replied sheepishly, "I'm one of those mediocre caregivers. I'm always embarrassed when I see people on Sunday morning and don't remember that their father is in the hospital or they lost their job. I always feel like I don't care enough."

"It's enough," June replied.

I went for a walk that afternoon and absorbed the thought that I had had an unrealistic view of compassion. There might be a healthy bit of awareness in my perceived self-centeredness. Perhaps the woman who dies with the most friends dies before her time (although I hope that never happens to June).

35. SERIOUS BUSINESS

IN THE BIBLE GOD sometimes used dreams to communicate with people. For example, in the story of Joseph and the coat of many colors, the butler, the baker, Pharaoh—even Joseph himself—had life-changing dreams. Thousands of years later, because of a dream, another Joseph gathered the courage to marry his pregnant fiancée, Mary.

God speaks to me through nature, friends, songs, scripture and sermons. Why not dreams? Especially ones I remember in vivid detail.

One night I dreamed Fred and I were guests at a resort in Baja, Mexico. At the airport ready to leave, I realized I hadn't packed my shoes. Also for some unknown reason, we had left without saying goodbye or thanking our hosts. I decided to go back to the hotel to retrieve my shoes and say goodbye. To get there quickly, I slid down a yellow fabric chute.

But when I exited the chute, I didn't know where I was. I asked a Mexican woman who was mopping a floor which direction led back to the airport. Tenderly, she put her hand on my shoulder, pointed out the door and said, "*Quattros, quattros horas.*" Four hours! She must be wrong.

I walked past kids laughing in the dusty streets and women buying mangoes and papayas in the market. I asked them for directions, but they replied, "*No entiendo Ingles.*"

Farther down the road a fat man in a pilot's uniform said, "Señora, don't worry. The planes are this way." He escorted me to a small local airport and couldn't understand why I was shaking my head.

An invisible line seemed to run north to south down this narrow peninsula that separated the poor Mexicans on one side from the resorts and international airport on the other. No roads connected the two sides.

An old black man unfolded a worn blanket making a nest for his wife and himself in an alcove by a cathedral. They offered to make space for me to spend the night with them, but I rushed past them up the church steps. There must be a passage to the other side in here, I thought.

The cathedral was dark and empty except for a cat and a girl who looked to be about twelve. The girl was kicking a soccer ball against the wall. I held a baby on my hip now. I don't know where he came from, nor did I know the time, but it was late. I kept hoping the girl would show me the way back to Fred, but she seemed unmoved by my anxiety. She ogled the baby and invited me to pet the cat. I asked her again if she knew the way to the airport, but she just pushed the ball in my direction.

That's when I woke up. I lay there for a long time wondering, like Pharaoh: what does this dream mean?

My spiritual director had attended a workshop on dreams; I thought she might be able to help. But the questions she asked seemed unimportant to me, and I batted them away.

She didn't give up. She listed the people in the dream and asked, "Do any of these people remind you of someone you know?"

None of them resembled anyone in my family, church, circle of friends, or childhood. Our hour ended. I paid her and left, convinced I had wasted my time and money.

The next morning I vented in my journal: *Who was the cleaning woman, the fellow at the airport, the black couple in the alcove, the baby? Who was the girl with the cat in the empty church? Why wouldn't she help me? I won't know the answers to these questions, God, unless you tell me.*

I began to pray, and immediately I knew who the people were. Jesus was the woman with the mop, the kids, the pilot. He was the old couple and the American hosts. He was the girl who wanted to play with me. My tears confirmed it was true.

A few days later a friend and I walked along Burrard Inlet in Port Moody. I told her about my dream and what happened after that. "How could I have been so thick? Any kid in Sunday School knows the answer to every question the teacher asks is Jesus."

She laughed, "You were pretty focused on getting back to . . . What were you trying to get back to anyway?"

"The North American seriously stressed-out life I'm used to, I suppose."

"And Jesus only wants to play with you. I like that."

"Me too, but I don't know how to do it."

In *New Seeds of Contemplation,* Thomas Merton suggested that God created the world and everything in it, so that Jesus would have a familiar place to descend to and kindred spirits to play with when he arrived. Merton writes, "What is serious to men is often trivial in the sight of God. What in God might appear to us as 'play' is perhaps what He Himself takes most seriously."[3]

Maybe that explains the baby on my hip. The dream occurred not long after my grandchildren were born. Those babies have taught me to enjoy endless variations of peek-a-boo. Once Hadrian laughed so hard he got the hiccups.

Back to my dream for a minute. You must be wondering about Fred. What did he do when I didn't make it back to the airport? Why did God allow us to be separated?

Once I woke up and thought about it, that didn't concern me in the least. I know Fred well enough to be certain he would come and find me. And he'd be delighted to join me in a world

---

[3] Thomas Merton, *New Seeds of Contemplation,* (New York, New Directions, 1961), 296.

that truly values an afternoon siesta. Nobody needs to teach him how to play.

But me? I have much to learn about the serious business of play.

36. ENGAGING IN SERIOUS BUSINESS

ACCORDING TO MY DREAM, Jesus wants to play with me. I asked him what that looks like, and he showed me how he plays with three of his friends.

I was biking along and I saw a fellow from our church installing a second story window. If I was driving my car, I would never pull over and stop on impulse, but on a bike, especially going uphill, sighting a friend is always a good reason to stop.

This guy is not much taller than me, about forty-five and balding. "Rapunzel, Rapunzel," I called out before I could help myself.

"I would if I had any," he said, laughing.

We kibitzed for a while about his current project. "I could be making ten times the money if I got more jobs and contracted out," he said. "But then I'd be driving around all day, constantly on the phone, home late, cranky."

He paused. "Hang on, I'll be right down." When he got down to the sidewalk, he lowered his voice. Now we were talking man-to-pastor. "I've been getting up half an hour early every morning—"

To pray?

"—to work on the car in my garage. It's peaceful. I don't take calls; I sip my coffee, tinker on the engine. And when I do, my day is incredibly smooth. I'm nice to my wife and my co-workers. Yesterday I was on the roof of this house—I hate being up there—and I wanted to lift my hands and praise God. That's not like me. Who'd a thought?"

A young couple in our church got married a few weeks ago. A close friend of both the bride and the groom's families, agreed to help decorate the church and assist with the stand-up reception for over two hundred people. This woman is a high school teacher who carefully allocates spare time between her husband and grown children, as well as friends, outreach work, and at least one knitting project.

The day before the wedding, she worked busily to set up the sanctuary and foyer while three musicians practiced their classical pieces. She puttered about laying out the tablecloths and deciding what would go where to the accompaniment of a piano, cello, and violin.

On the wedding day, three hours before the guests arrived, the trio had one last rehearsal. The violinist told me later she thought she heard someone enter the sanctuary. When she looked up, she saw the woman swaying and moving to Pachelbel's Canon. The music that had collected in her body the day before could not be contained.

"Jump? Jump?" my two-year-old grandson, Hadrian, said and climbed on the bed I was making. I held him under his arms while he laughed and bounced as high as he could. When I gave him an extra boost into the air, he shrieked with delight.

"Mo-re. Mo-re," he begged, and we did it again.

Of course being the person I am, I analyze how play works. These three players did what they loved to do. The certain type of play one engaged in may not satisfy another—though I could imagine both adults as bed jumpers in their early years. From what I observed, playing with Jesus is easy. Who can resist it when he winks and says, "Let's go"?

Now that I think about it, I've had those invitations. Ever since we were first married, Fred and I dreamed of living aboard a boat and sailing across an ocean or two. When we had finally saved enough money to do it, we soberly considered what a foolish venture this would be. We could list a dozen reasons why we should act more responsibly, and people underscored those reasons whenever they found us reading a book on offshore cruising.

But whenever I closed my eyes and asked Jesus what he wanted us to do, I saw my Savior with a silly grin on his face saying, "Let's go!"

And we did. From 1992-95 Fred, Rudy, Heidi and I spent three years sailing west around the world to Turkey.

That was twenty years ago, and since then I seemed to have forgotten how to have fun. But Jesus hasn't. He's seriously into play. Lately he's been showing up everywhere I go, making work into fun. I suspect he thinks even cleaning the bathroom could be enjoyable, if we did it together. He hasn't quite sold me on that one, but I have a feeling he won't give up trying.

37. TRUST ME

WHEN RUDY AND HEIDI were young, our family used to play a board game called *Trust Me*. In that game, when your playing piece lands on a square with a tiny plastic briefcase on it—No Takers Acres on Green Horn Avenue, for example—you can invest in that company. At the end of the game, the brief cases are turned over, and the truth is revealed: dollar signs or the fateful words, "You've been had!"

When God plays with me the way Jesus welcomed children on his knee, that's great. But when God plays games with me, it's a whole different story.

A few weeks ago, God and I played a variation of *Trust Me* called *How Slow Can I Make the Skytrain Run and Still Get You to the Bus on Time?*

That day I had a meeting twenty miles away. According to the weather forecast, this would be the last clear day before a cold, wet front set in. So I decided to take my bike, Gracie, with me and travel there by Skytrain and bus, then bicycle home. The crucial part of the equation was getting a bus which runs hourly. I allowed seven minutes to make my connection.

I biked to the Skytrain and arrived a few minutes early. While I waited for the train, a thought occurred to me: what if I get to the bus, but its bike rack's already full? I was about to abort my plan and take the car when the train arrived. I got on and checked the time: it was five minutes late.

I still believed I might make it when we abruptly stopped outside the station where I needed to transfer trains. Three long minutes later, the train began to move again and pulled into the station. I hurried off the train and waited for the painstakingly slow elevator to arrive. I reformulated my plan: whichever train comes first—the one going over the river or the one going back home—is the one I'll take. I heard the train coming and picked up Gracie, thankful she's so light. I ran up the stairs and boarded the outgoing train.

The next stop was where I needed to catch the bus. I grabbed Gracie, bounded down the stairs and discovered the bus loop was on the other side of a barricaded street. I had to go back up the stairs and down the other side. There was my bus with one space left on its bike rack. Don't go, I pleaded under my breath.

I plunked Gracie down in front of the bus, making it impossible for the driver to leave. But he was reading a magazine and hardly noticed me. I was panting as I got on the bus and fed my ticket into the machine. There were only two other passengers on board which led me to suspect that the bus I wanted to catch had already left. But as soon as I sat down, the driver closed the door, and we left the station.

I peeled off my jacket and fleece vest. Slowly my temperature, breathing, and heart rate returned to normal. I was relieved to have made it, but I didn't feel like I'd won this round of *Trust Me*. If I missed the bus, the briefcase would say, "You should have been more prepared." Now that I caught the bus, the brief case seemed to say, "See, you should have trusted me." It wasn't a fair game; either way, God wins and I lose. I wanted to scream.

Two weeks later I was at Rivendell again, walking the labyrinth. With each step I was consciously aware that God was present—not merely looking on in the silence, but actively involved in it. The labyrinth's stones reminded me of the squares on the *Trust Me* board and the game God played with me on transit.

But as I walked slowly in the silence, I saw that game in a different light: no matter what happened *I* was the winner. If I caught the bus, I would have arrived on time. If I missed it, God would have taken me on a different adventure.

At the center of the labyrinth, I looked down at the pattern of a flower. Six white flat rocks encircled a seventh. I crouched down and placed my palm and outstretched fingers on its cool surface, as if it were a window and God's hand matched mine on the other side.

Thank you.

Where can I go from your Spirit?
Where can I flee from your presence?
If I go up to the heavens, you are there;
if I make my bed in the depths, you are there.
If I rise on the wings of the dawn,
if I settle on the far side of the sea,
even there your hand will guide me,
your right hand will hold me fast.
—Psalm 139:7-10

38. PILLARS OF SALT

With the coming of dawn, the angels urged Lot, saying, "Hurry! Take your wife and your two daughters who are here, or you will be swept away when the city is punished. Flee for your lives! Don't look back, and don't stop anywhere in the plain! Flee to the mountains or you will be swept away!"

But Lot's wife looked back, and she became a pillar of salt.

—Genesis 19:15, 17, 26

WHEN I THINK OF Lot's wife being turned into a pillar of salt, I ask myself, what made her do it? Was she abandoning a lover? Was she curious, afraid, or glad those nasty people got what they deserved? Did she look back out of compassion and doubt God's? Maybe she was leaving behind a precious stash of yarn, an unfinished novel, or a perfectly manicured garden and wanted one last glimpse at her azaleas. Maybe she looked back because she had been told not to. Whatever the reason—zap—she ceased to be.

For weeks now I've been processing something I read. "If the good news is that we are found in Christ, it must also be true that being lost is a real possibility."[4] This sentence, written by Alan Jones, an Episcopal priest and spiritual director, comes after he writes that our beloved God is "actively seeking us out," transforming us, and "drawing us into a wider relationship with

---

[4] Alan Jones, *Exploring Spiritual Direction* (New York, NY: The Seabury Press, 1982), 20.

him."[5] This God I heartily embrace, but the other one, the one who allows us to be lost, makes me uncomfortable. I don't want to believe I can be lost, but Jones holds the possibility in front of me, and so does the writer of Genesis.

In my theological studies, I learned that the Old Testament view held God responsible for everything that happened.[6] For example, when Pharaoh stubbornly and repeatedly refused to let God's people leave Egypt for the Promised Land, Moses, the writer of Exodus, said God hardened Pharaoh's heart. Not for a moment would Moses have considered this sadistic king an innocent victim in a divine power play. Moses was simply implying that God was not undone by Pharaoh's hardheartedness. Centuries later when the Israelites told and retold the stories of the Exodus, even though they said "God hardened Pharaoh's heart," no one blamed God for Pharaoh's actions.

God's constant desire is to save not condemn. Over and over, when the Israelites hurt and oppressed others, God sent prophets to help them recognize the error of their ways. Untiringly God forgave and restored them. The Apostle Paul, in his letter to the Romans, says God's mercy is so great that it sometimes appears unjust because God shows mercy to those who don't deserve it.[7]

Even though some Bible stories portray God as overly harsh, I remind myself: this is not God's character. There must be more to the story that I don't understand. There has to be because Jesus, who is the exact representation of God, didn't zap sinners; he befriended them.

Perhaps God's judgment is more descriptive than prescriptive. In other words when we turn away from God, we aren't being punished, but as Jones says, we lose ourselves. When

---

[5] Ibid p. 2
[6] Frederic W. Bush, *Ruth/Esther World Biblical Commentary*. (Dallas, Texas: Word Books, 1996), 106.
[7] Romans 9:14, 15

we turn away from the source of our humanity, we are no longer at peace with ourselves or with others. Just as the moon has no light apart from the sun, we have no humanity apart from God, in whose image we were created.

I don't like knowing that the more I turn away from God, the less human I become. But this Bible story spells it out for me in no uncertain terms: if I keep turning away from Love, I will become as hard as a pillar of salt.

How I long to keep turning to my Beloved who fills me with compassion. I grieve that I have turned away from God so many times. But under my grief stirs the hope, that in each returning, there is a greening of my humanity.

39. REASON TO PAUSE

ONE MORNING AFTER I finished praying with half a dozen women in a church basement, I went to use the restroom. When I opened the door, I was shocked to discover a man inside—thankfully fully clothed. I avoided eye contact, mumbled an apology and discovered, to my amazement, a women's restroom right next to it. Later I recalled seeing a male symbol on the first door seconds before I opened it. I wished I had paused long enough to take in that vital piece of information.

Not pausing to read signs must have been the week's theme. That Friday I rode my bike to Ethical Bean to pick up our church's coffee order. As I rode past their offices and coffee shop, I noticed a shoe brush had been installed at the entrance but thought little of it. Because the usual door I entered around back was locked, I walked my bike in through the loading bay between a stack of empty coffee bags and the roaster. This was nothing new. I'd taken my bike in before, but now the employees had green lab coats over their street clothes, and some had surgical masks on.

The shipper/receiver caught sight of me. "You can't bring that bike in here! You're not even supposed to be in here. New health regulations." He ignored my apologies and escorted me out. "That's why we installed the doorbell."

The heavy metal door slammed shut in my face. That's when I saw a black and white sign which read: "Ring bell for service."

After I left, I hoped he didn't have to stop what he was doing to disinfect the floor. If only I had paused and read the sign.

That weekend I returned to Rivendell. Once again the labyrinth helped me understand what God was doing. As I walked, the path kept changing direction. Mindful of this, at every turn I stopped to look around me. Each time I did, I enjoyed a slightly different view—of the trees, of the lodge above, and of the harbor below. But I had to pause to see it.

God led me, step by step, into the labyrinth's center. Before I was led out again, we paused many times to change direction.

God invites me to do the same in my everyday life. A phone call interrupted my sermon preparation but yielded the valuable insight that I needed. A rainy day slowed me down and gave me rest. When I paused to take in how tired a friend was, I chose to ask her about her day, instead of insisting that she hear about mine.

I don't like changing course once I've made a plan. But I'd rather alter my course than ignore a friend or be found red-faced on the wrong side of the door.

Your hand will guide me.
—Psalm 139:10

40. OPEN MY EYES

JESUS TALKED MORE ABOUT the Kingdom of God than anything else. He proclaimed that it was both coming and already here. So I asked Jesus to show me where his kingdom has come. Open my eyes, Lord. Let me see what you are doing here on earth, I prayed silently, while Fred and I were shopping at Mountain Equipment Co-op one day.

I looked around at the shoppers and merchandise and expected something to pop out at me. Miraculously a sign appeared. It said, "Organic cotton hoodies on sale for only $19.99."

I love a bargain, but when I imagined myself in one of those neon pink sweatshirts, I concluded that buying one was not God's plan for my life. In the line-up at the checkout, I said to Fred, "Get this. They're selling organic cotton clothing. What's up with that? You can't eat it."

"No, but the pesticides used to grow cotton are killing the soil. I hate to think of what it does to the farmers."

I recalled riding our bikes past an Okanagan farm worker. He was dressed head to toe in protective gear while he sprayed an apple crop. Fred had hollered, "Pedal faster. You don't want to breathe in that stuff."

After our trip to MEC, I learned more about growing cotton. A single crop of cotton is sprayed with pesticides up to twenty times. Much of the cotton we buy in Canada comes from China or India where most farmers do not have access to protective gear nor are they taught how to handle these hazardous chemicals. I pictured the runoff from the poisoned fields flowing into the streams that Indian families used as their water supply. According to the World Health Organization, twenty thousand people in developing countries die each year of pesticide poisoning. As if that isn't bad enough, after several years of growing cotton the land becomes unusable.

Organizations like the Sustainable Cotton Project in California provide farmers with the education and support needed to grow organic cotton successfully. Among other things, they instruct farmers to allow the land to lie fallow periodically, the way the Hebrews did in Old Testament times. In Leviticus, God directed people to let the fields lie fallow once every seven years. I hadn't paid much attention to this Levitical law, but now I see how important it is. God was already at work helping us fulfill the command given to Adam and Eve to care for the earth.

Centuries later Jesus commanded his disciples to love God and love our neighbor. This doesn't mean we put away our gardening tools and move on to more important work. Jesus said these two commands sum up all the others.

I live in a second story condominium, and the only gardening I think about is metaphorical: pruning bad habits or growing fruit of the Spirit. When I asked Jesus to show me how I could participate in his kingdom work, I never expected him to be this practical—or blunt as to suggest, that buying conventionally grown cotton could make me an accomplice to death and destruction.

Yikes, Lord! I feel like I'd been hit with a two-by-four. I get it: buying organics isn't just a nice thing to do; it's a way we usher in God's kingdom. Whether I liked it or not, my eyes were opened. What I buy affects my neighbors and impacts their land.

I resolved the clothing problem by shopping in thrift stores. But what about food choices? Organic produce is at least double the price of conventionally farmed fruits and vegetables. This was not going to be easy. Many times I began a shopping trip with good intentions but returned without a single organic item. Finally I stopped shopping alone and brought along a support team. Whenever I put an organic item in my cart, I imagined millions of admirers from around the world applauding me. Organic farmers and retailers saluted me. Future generations of healthy children cheered. The trees of the fields clapped their hands; the lilies in the valleys nodded their heads. Even my body sighed with relief when I bought food and clothing that sustained the earth.

I wish I could say that rising to the status of hero was enough to convert my behavior. But this new undertaking was not only costing more money, but more time as well. I needed to read labels and ask questions about where and how things were produced. I had to consider the environmental impact of buying organic produce imported from other countries versus supporting local farmers. Some of these farms, although not certified organic, use few pesticides or none at all. It also took time to shop around; I couldn't find all the food I wanted in one place—at least not on our income.

In the midst of my conundrum, I received an anonymous gift of three hundred dollars. I didn't know why it was given, but I knew what God wanted me to do with the money: spend it on organics.

The next time I went shopping, organic grapefruits "happened" to be on sale. I bought a bag of them. That evening I grabbed one and planned to eat it while I read. But Jesus wanted me to close the book and enjoy the grapefruit with him. *It's my gift to you*, he seemed to say.

I sat back in my chair and dug my thumb into the thick peel. A citrus mist tickled my nose. I savored the grapefruit, section by tangy section, stopping now and then to lick the juice that trickled onto my wrist. As I held the fragrant peels in my hands, all I wanted to do was live generously and kindly.

41. WHAT MY BODY KNOWS

"I'VE BEEN GOING TO a fitness class at the gym," I told my spiritual director one afternoon. "The instructor wants us to know and feel each muscle we are working. At first I tuned out and got the hour over with. But lately I've sensed that Jesus wants me to pay attention to what I'm doing and to offer that hour to God as prayer. So I'm trying to feel my body and listen to it."

As soon as those words left my mouth, warmth flooded my chest and brought tears to my eyes. I stopped talking and paid attention to my body. The warmth flowed into my shoulders and relaxed them. It travelled down my arms like a wave of peace.

"Listening to my body seems to be very important to God," I said.

There's a saying that "the mind deceives, but the body never lies." I can find evidence to support that statement. My mind may convince me that an extra piece of pizza will do me no harm, but my body reveals the truth when I have to loosen my belt a notch. Fatigue tells me when I need to take a break. My skin tingles when I am delighted. My stomach tightens when I'm afraid. And when warmth rises up in me and brings me to tears, like it did that day, it usually means something is true. Not only that, God wants me to know that it's true.

This reminds me of John Wesley, the circuit-riding Episcopal clergyman who founded Methodism. In his early life, he feared he would never be good enough for God. That changed one evening in 1738 when he unwillingly went to a reading of Luther's preface to the Epistle to the Romans. Wesley wrote in his journal, "About a quarter before nine, while he was describing the change which God works in the heart through faith in Christ, I felt my heart strangely warmed. I felt I did trust in Christ, Christ alone, for salvation; and an assurance was given me that he had taken away my sins, even mine, and saved me from the law of sin and death."

Wesley's body convinced him in a way that his mind never could.

The two disciples walking to Emmaus the day Jesus rose from the dead had a similar experience. They met Jesus on the road and invited him to join them, but for some reason they were kept from recognizing him. Bewildered and heartbroken over recent events, the travelers told this stranger about the crucifixion of their rabbi and friend, the one they thought was the Messiah. Jesus listened. Then, quoting scripture after scripture, he explained how God had planned it all, including the Messiah's resurrection.

That evening when Jesus broke the bread and gave it to them, their eyes were opened. They saw their Lord alive and in their midst. Afterwards they said to each other, "Were not our hearts burning within us while he talked with us on the road and opened the Scriptures to us?" While their minds were confused and their hearts overwhelmed, their bodies bore witness to the risen Lord.

These historical accounts make me want to show my skin and bones a little more respect. But like many Christians, I am at odds with my body. I can't dance, and unlike Eric Liddle in *Chariots of Fire*, I don't "feel God's pleasure when I run," just aches and pains. I treat my body as little more than a vehicle that gets me from here to there. When it makes odd noises, I turn up the radio, down more coffee as if it's motor oil, and keep on truckin'. I begrudge the effort it takes to look after myself, and I'm afraid that if I give my body too much attention, it will get me into trouble. Honestly, I am much more at ease with ideas and feelings than I am with what I see in the mirror.

But God loves my body. It's not easy for me to say that out loud, but God does. It's Christ's home and the temple where his Spirit lives. God loves it from bumper to bumper.

I bless God when I take care of my body, and the Spirit is over the moon with delight when I listen to it. For my body knows my Triune God in a way my mind and heart never will. My body knew, long before I did, that I was created in the image of the Trinity. The Father, Son and Spirit are different but equally sacred, and so are my mind, heart *and* body.

Do you not know that your bodies are temples of the Holy Spirit, who is in you, whom you have received from God?
—1 Corinthians 6:19

42. BRANCHES WIDE AND OPEN

IN THE SUMMER OF a long, difficult year, Fred and I spent two weeks in Banff National Park. Beneath Castle Mountain, we found a quiet campsite with sunlight and shade as well as trees perfectly spaced for Fred's hammock. A little brook ran along one side giving us space from our neighbor. Every morning we packed a lunch and set out to hike in alpine meadows, cycle the Bow Valley Parkway, or soak in hot springs with tourists from around the world. Every afternoon we returned to our quiet little nest in the woods.

I hoped I would be able to hold onto the peace I'd found while camping in the Rockies, but within a week of being home again, not a shred of it remained. I kept losing my keys and forgetting things. I was distracted in prayer and uninspired by scripture. God seemed so far away that I began to suspect our vacation had not helped much.

But something had changed: my relationship with trees. I now found them in the foreground. I passed maples, as I have done a thousand times on my walk to work, and was awestruck by their vibrant green leaves. Near the creek another one held out a thick straight branch as if it were inviting me to climb it. In our friend's yard, a fire-red sugar maple hushed my soul and hallowed the ground.

One Friday afternoon, spruce and cedar trees listened to my thoughts as I biked the Central Valley Greenway into Vancouver. That morning a friend I hadn't seen in a while dropped off a book I had loaned her. I wasn't busy at the time and considered inviting her in for tea. But when I heard her knock, I didn't answer the door. She ended up leaving the book in the breezeway.

We're supposed to love our neighbors, I thought as I rode along, but I push people away. My heart beat in my stomach, and tears clouded my eyes.

On Main Street I stopped for coffee. A young man with dreadlocks and piercings rinsed my travel mug and filled it with a dark, fair trade brew. It smelled heavenly. I looked for a place to sit down, but the chairs were occupied. I put the mug into my pannier and continued riding until I found a park with plenty of grass and a stout leafy oak. I leaned Gracie against the tree and sat in its shade.

As I drank my coffee, I remembered the Welcoming Prayer. It invited me to welcome "what is" with branches wide and open. I thought about what is and what isn't my life. I thought about how long I have prayed for things that never seem to change. As I thought about it all, I began to weep. And God was there, like the oak, silent and strong.

Chestnut trees ushered me home; branches touched overhead playing London Bridge with me along the Tenth Avenue bike route. On the Greenway, Mountain Ash held out their orange-berried branches like Italian mamas wanting to put color in my cheeks. And when I walked Gracie up the driveway, I saw two girls lying on the lawn. They rested their heads on the bony roots of a maple and talked about everything and nothing.

Welcoming Prayer

*Gently become aware of your body and your interior state.
Welcome, welcome, welcome.
I welcome everything that comes to me in this moment
because I know it is for my healing.
I welcome all thoughts, feelings, emotions, persons, situations
and conditions.*

*I let go of my desire for security.
I let go of my desire for approval.
I let go of my desire for control.
I let go of my desire to change any situation, condition,
person, or myself.*

*I open to the love and presence of God and the healing
action and grace within.*

—Cathy McCarthy, *Welcoming Prayer*

43. LEGLESS IN A DUMPSTER

help me
I shout again
throat raw
body crumpled
against cold steel and cardboard

ants scale to freedom
without breaking a sweat
ants
I could crush with one finger
save themselves
but I can't

a thousand inner voices
judge
sentence
mock me

I holler
Christ   can you hear me?
are you there?

I've seen you around
you were here
homeless
dirty

stubbly beard and broken shoes
I saw you sort through trash
for gems and
when you found one you
moistened it with your breath
polished it with your shirt and
wrapped it in bits of cloth
as if it were a newborn

I wait for you to grip
the rim of hell with your left hand
lean down and grab hold
of me with your right
then
with a grunt that splits the atom
hoist me up
and out of here

I watch the moon rise
count the stars
and look for you
through a crack in the corner

44. PEACE DANCING

SEPTEMBER 1998 I RECEIVED a phone call from my brother. "She left me," he said and began to cry. As he filled in the details, a new reality unfolded, and there was no folding it back to the way things were before.

"I wish you weren't so far away," I said, wiping the tears from my cheeks.

"Me too," he said. "I might need to call a lot."

"That's okay," I replied.

Once or twice a week, my brother phoned. He'd talk and cry until he was too tired to say any more. And I'd listen, two thousand miles from his pain.

A couple of months after his wife left him, my brother went for counseling. He told me about the sessions when he called. I listened, fascinated by what I heard. But then he asked me a question, and all of a sudden it wasn't just about him anymore

"The counselor wanted to hear about our childhood," he said. "I told her I didn't remember Mom or Dad ever holding us. Do you?"

"Not really."

"The counselor thought that was sad."

"Hmm," I said and looked up to see Fred pointing at his watch. "Oh, man. It's 9:30! I'd better go or I'll be late for work. I love you."

"I love you too," he said.

I grabbed my bag, kissed Fred goodbye and drove to East Vancouver through the slushy snow. Just before ten, I arrived at the group home for my overnight shift.

I pushed the phone call from my mind and went about my duties. But when I climbed into bed, I thought about what my brother had said. There was no getting around it: though my parents did their best, my siblings and I did not receive the affection we longed for as children. The counselor's validation made me weep. And once I started crying, I couldn't stop. Finally I fell asleep with a song by Rich Mullins playing in my head:

> *Hold me Jesus 'cause I'm shaking like a leaf*
> *You have been King of my glory*
> *Won't you be my Prince of Peace?*[8]

The next morning as I helped Helen pick out clothes for church, she asked me if I felt better. She must have heard me crying.

Once I got home, there was the usual rush getting our young family fed and out the door. We arrived at church while the congregation was singing the first verse of "O Come, O Come Emmanuel." Then a woman I knew came in with her family. She brought her four-month-old daughter in a car seat and set her down on the floor at the back of the church while she hung up her coat.

I crouched down in front of the baby and put on a smile. "I hear you're playing baby Jesus in this year's Christmas pageant," I said. "Feeling up to the part?"

The baby stared back at me with ancient eyes as if she too knew I was grieving. She curled her fingers around one of mine

---

[8] "Hold Me, Jesus" by Rich Mullins, *A Liturgy, a Legacy & a Ragamuffin Band*, 1993. Reunion Records.

and looked at me. At that moment it seemed as if she really was Jesus, and he was holding me. I felt comforted.

The mom thanked me for watching her daughter, picked up her child and joined the congregation. I stood there savoring the joy resting inside me.

I remember that moment as if it were yesterday; the memory is as crisp and clear as Christmas Day.

"I bring you good news of great joy," the angel told the shepherds that first Christmas. "The Savior has been born." The shepherds left their flocks and found baby Jesus wrapped in cloths, laying in a manger, and knelt down and worshipped him. They went home rejoicing, peace dancing in their souls.

We too rejoice, for Jesus has come into our world, into our lives, and into our grief with tidings of comfort and joy.

Peace is joy resting, and joy is peace dancing.
—Charles Haddon Spurgeon

45. HALF

I WAS READING A book on Sabbath rest when a thought interrupted me—a complete sentence in fact, directed at me. It was so clear that I immediately attributed it to God. It certainly wasn't something I invented; I never would have said such a thing. I heard, *You could do half of what you're doing.*

What? Was God really suggesting that half of what I do is unnecessary? What half was I supposed to give up? I didn't think God expected me to quit my job at the church a few months after my hours were increased. I didn't think I should stop offering spiritual direction; it's where I come alive. What then? The gym, Gracie, my writing? I knew what half I'd like to give up— housework—but somehow I didn't think that's what God had in mind. This statement made such little sense to me that I didn't even record it in my journal. But I didn't forget it either.

A month later I was biking to see my spiritual director and considered what I might talk about. I had narrowed it down to a couple of concerns, but in the silence after she lit the candle, what landed in my lap was that whimsical sentence. I still didn't think it was such a big deal until I said it out loud and began to cry—a sure sign that this was a big deal to God.

"What's going on for you?" my director asked.

"Our lead pastor's on vacation, which means I'm the pastor on call. I'm preaching four weeks in a row, and you know how absorbing the creative process is for me. Meanwhile, I still need to make pastoral visits, solve problems, and listen to people who show up and want to talk. I don't have a spare moment anywhere, and I constantly feel like I'm short-changing people. To add to this, Fred and I promised my brothers we would cycle a good chunk of the Oregon coast with them. When do I have time to train for that? On the bike ride here, I didn't have much energy. I don't know if I'll be able to do it."

"When you hear yourself say this, does anything come to mind?"

I thought of an image God gave one of my directees a few days before. "She told me that she pictured God marching around the fortress protecting her heart, like Joshua circling the walls of Jericho. When I picture God doing the same thing for me, I feel peaceful."

"How so?"

"I don't want this wall around my heart, and it makes me feel better to know that God is going to bring it down. That it's not my job."

"And what do you hope will happen when this wall comes down?"

"I'll have space," I said and could feel my chest expanding. "And yet, when I imagine myself without those thick walls around me, I feel exposed . . . vulnerable and weak."

"What might God be saying about that?"

I paused to think about her question. "That it's okay to be weak. It's okay to let the wall come down."

"When you think of that wall, how it's constructed of big stones, do you have a sense of what those stones might be?"

I closed my eyes and pictured the intimidating wall. "They're monuments to me: the things I do so people will think well of me. I want to be good at everything, even Scrabble. I want to be a good pastor, a good friend, a good grandmother, so I do whatever anyone wants me to. I like my monuments, but the cost of maintaining them is squeezing the life out of me."

"What is God inviting you to do?"

"To let them crumble," I replied, drawing a breath of freedom. "Be weak—and ordinary."

"And what might that look like?"

"I could give up trying to live up to my own expectations. I don't have to ride the whole way in Oregon. I could ride half the distance each day and let my sister-in-law pick me up in the van."

"You could," she said, suppressing a smile.

"I could," I said, biting my lip.

On the bike ride home, I thought about what it would be like to embrace my weaknesses. Could I preach an ordinary sermon? Could I refrain from making casseroles for new moms, and feel secure when others get the accolades I covet?

In the next two weeks, I lost at Scrabble twice in a row and chalked it up to God bringing down another monument. I laughed about it, even mentioned my losses in a sermon.

But once I was on vacation, Gracie and I hit the pavement with a vengeance. And every time I pictured myself on the Oregon coast bike trip with my brothers, not once did I see myself riding in the van.

46. SURFIN' USA

FRED AND I SAT contented on the beach and listened to the surf. We gazed at the ships on the horizon and watched kids and dogs—and surfers riding the waves.

"Doesn't that make you want to get a board and go surfing?" he asked.

Neither of us had surfed before. When we were first married over thirty years ago, we used to scuba dive. I know how much work it is to get into and out of a wetsuit. Then I considered the energy it would take to paddle through the surf, energy I wanted to save for cycling.

We had come to Oregon to cycle 250 miles of the coast with my siblings. A month before our vacation, both of us caught colds that dragged on for weeks and put us behind in our training. I was concerned that we might not have the stamina for it. Fred still had the occasional cough.

All this whooshed through my mind in less than ten seconds before I spit out a solitary "No" to his question. Fred said nothing more.

A few days later, we were on the beach again. We leaned against driftwood, and watched the surfers. Fred said, "You know, you can rent a wetsuit and surfboard for twenty-four hours for only forty dollars." Then it hit me. Whenever Fred asks me if *I'd* like to do something, like he did a few days earlier, he really means *he'd* like to do it.

We checked out the surf shop in Manzanita with the advertised deal. They had plenty of boards and a suit in his size.

On our bike ride back to the campground, I made one final appeal. "At least talk to somebody who knows what they're doing and find out what you're in for." Once again Fred was silent.

The next day was sunny and hot. I biked to Oswald West State Park while Fred drove to the surf shop. We agreed to meet at the parking lot that led to Falcon Beach, a Mecca for surfers.

Half way up a long hill, when my calves were begging me to get off and walk, our black Mazda passed by with a surfboard lashed to the roof. Fred waved through the open sunroof window.

From the parking lot, we carried the surfboard down the half mile long trail to the beach. "It's heavier than I thought it would be," he said, and we put it down periodically to catch our breath.

On the beach, I huddled in the shade while Fred put on the wet suit, complete with mitts and a hood. He posed for some photos; then off he went. But he was back again ten minutes later. "The current's taking me too far south," he said. "I'm going farther up the beach."

He paddled out, ducked the waves, and paddled some more. At one point I lost track of him. When I caught sight of him again, he was standing up. I threw my arms in the air and as soon as I let out a "Woo-hoo!" I realized it wasn't Fred after all but another man with the same color surfboard.

Precisely one hour after he started, Fred announced, "I'm done," and plopped down on the sand.

The next morning at breakfast, Fred said, "I still can't believe I went surfing."

I wondered if lying on and falling off a surfboard a number of times qualified as surfing, but I kept that thought to myself. "I'm glad you didn't injure yourself," I said.

"Oh, I forgot to tell you. Some guy saw the surfboard on our car and asked me how the surfing was. I told him I didn't know. It was the first time I ever tried it. 'Oh, then,' the man says. 'The correct answer is: It was the best day surfing I ever had in my life.'"

And I could see by the smile on Fred's face that it was.

This is the day the LORD has made;
let us rejoice and be glad in it.
—Psalm 118:24 (NRSV)

47. LET GO

There remains, then, a Sabbath-rest for the people of God; for those who enter God's rest also rest from their own work, just as God did from his. Let us, therefore, make every effort to enter that rest. —Hebrews 4:9-11

"A BEAUTIFUL DAY FOR a bike ride," the counselor said, noticing the helmet in my hand. She invited me to sit down. "How are you and Fred doing?"

"We're fine," I said. "We biked a big section of the Oregon coast this summer with two of my brothers. I wasn't sure if we'd be able to bike sixty miles a day four days in a row, but we did."

"I can't even imagine doing that."

"Well, Fred was pretty bagged afterwards. All spring he'd been saying he didn't like bike rides over thirty miles. But on the trip, whenever I reminded him of that, he said he felt fine."

"Of course he did. He wanted to be with you guys. Who wants to admit they're getting older and can't do what they used to? We need to get beat up a few times before we really believe our bodies can't do it anymore."

"Well, I wish he would figure it out. When he pushes himself and tries to do too much, he gets grouchy and isn't much fun to live with."

We talked for a while about how that makes me feel and what I might do about it. Then she asked, "And how are you doing?"

"All right. Too busy, though. I want to do it all. I say yes to everything. Then I'm upset if the least little thing goes wrong or if people don't keep up their end of the housework," I said. "I hate finding other people's dishes in the sink."

"So when you do too much you get . . . grouchy?"

I knew then how my busyness affected Fred and Heidi. "Yeah," I admitted sheepishly, "I guess I'm no fun to live with at times either."

"Nobody is. That's why we have to let go of some things. Even things we really enjoy. And when we do, we grieve their loss."

I ruminated on what she'd said while I rode home. I had thought that I could manage whatever I squeezed into my schedule and didn't realize the toll busyness was taking.

Almost daily I asked God to help me be more loving and kind, and I kept wondering when that prayer would be answered. Now it was. I couldn't help but see God's hand in this. Kindness takes energy. If I say yes to everything, I don't have energy left to be kind.

As I neared home, I knew I'd have to rush to get showered and eat dinner before going out again. Saturday was fully booked; then there was church Sunday morning, a baby shower in the afternoon, and our monthly get together with girlfriends that evening. I didn't want to give up any of those things, but when I looked at the coming week, there was no Sabbath rest ahead.

"I didn't go to the baby shower," I said to my friends after I told them what happened in counseling. "I spent the afternoon hanging out with Fred. But I know that when I hear about the baby shower, I'm going to wish I'd been there. I hate missing anything."

"I didn't go either," one woman said, "and I felt guilty."

"You know, I used to think that if I did the things God wanted me to and let go of the others, I'd feel good about it," I said.

They laughed and nodded.

"It sounds crazy, but I believed it."

"I think we all did," another said.

Eventually I told Fred about the counseling session. He had a good laugh and made me tell Heidi. She smiled as she continued washing the dishes I'd left in the sink.

48. SOMETHING EXTRA

I WAS ALMOST ASLEEP when I remembered that next week was Homelessness Action Week. I had promised Wanda Mulholland of the Burnaby Task Force on Homelessness that our church would do something extra that Wednesday.

Back then we served soup alongside Progressive Housing Society's outreach van at a nearby Skytrain station, instead of at the church where we do now. That meant our volunteers had to load up their vehicles with pots, cups, crackers, utensils, a camp stove, and propane tank in order to heat up and serve two ice cream buckets full of homemade soup. I couldn't ask them to do any more. I shot a "Help!" heavenward and went to sleep.

Tuesday morning I awoke determined to fulfill my promise. Of course I could always do something myself. I could set up a second camp stove and make grilled cheese sandwiches or throw together some chicken Caesar wraps; those are popular. But I have done it myself enough times to know that if I keep doing it myself, I'll get worn out. When I worked in children's ministry many years ago, my mentor told me, "God uses people to bring the kingdom, but God won't always use you." I remember feeling deflated at the time; now I appreciate her wisdom.

Okay, God, who can help us?

Mid-morning one of the workers at New Life's Community Free Store told me that Ken had dropped in. "He brought two huge bags of kids' clothes and a bunch of toys and books. Really nice stuff," she said. "Oh, and he told me to tell you he's bringing hot dogs on Wednesday when they serve soup."

"Did he mean tomorrow or next Wednesday?" I asked.

"I don't know. He didn't say."

Back in my office, I found Ken's card in a desk drawer. Ken used to run an electronics shop in the neighbourhood of my previous church. While I had packed up our weekly kids' club, Ken would arrive after work to put coffee on for a group that met in the church basement. We'd shoot the breeze.

Years later the Free Store workers raved about a man named Ken who dropped by from time to time with donations of clothes for the store or food for our outreach. This saint even carted off the unusable clothing to get recycled, so it wouldn't end up in the landfill. I kept hearing about this generous fellow but was never around to meet him. Then one day I saw him in the church parking lot; I recognized his neatly trimmed beard and mile wide grin.

Ken rolled down the window of his van. "This is where you've been hiding out. How the hell are you anyway?" Before he drove away, he handed me the card I held in my hand.

"I was at your church this morning, brought a big load of clothes," Ken said over the phone. "Somebody down the street had a garage sale. Wondered what to do with the stuff that didn't sell. I said, 'I'll take it.'"

"Sounds like you were in the right place at the right time." I said. "Hey, I hear you're bringing hot dogs Wednesday."

"Yup, *next* Wednesday for Homelessness Action Week."

"You're an answer to prayer, you know. I told Wanda we'd do something extra, but I couldn't ask our volunteers to do any more."

Ken laughed. "Well, you tell them not to worry. I'll bring the dogs and plenty of coffee too."

I breathed a sigh of relief. We had something extra to serve, even though we had nothing more to give.

49. A VOICE ON THE PERIPHERY

"When are you preaching again?" a friend asked me over coffee.

"Not until the new year."

"Not till then? But you love preaching."

"I know, but I feel like I need to slow down. I've decided not to lead the next prayer retreat either. That was a tough decision. I kept thinking I should do it. I wanted to and planned out. But whenever I was quiet, I sensed God out here—" and I extended my arm, "saying gently, 'But I don't want you to.'"

"Interesting that God is way out there and barely audible. Where's your voice?"

Tears came with the answer. "The part of me that wants to say no is out there too."

"The louder voice," I said, cupping my hands over my diaphragm "is right here and says yes to everything. It's full of energy and loves to be up front doing big things. This voice has been running the show for a long time. But lately I've begun to hear another voice, a still, small voice on the periphery asking me to do less."

"I know that voice," she said. "It's a loving one that notices when we take on too much. I'm glad you are paying attention to it."

"It's been a slow process, but whenever I listen to it, I am able to let go of something."

In fact during our conversation on the walk back to my friend's house, I thought of two more things I could let go of.

A few days later, another walk led me past a field with ripe cobs of corn. They spoke to me of patience and abundance. It had been four months since God had asked me to do half of what I was doing, and I had barely let go of a tenth. But somehow I sensed God was okay with that; God didn't expect me to change overnight. The Spirit was orchestrating things as beautifully as the corn being grown for the harvest. Here was that still, small voice again, this time allowing me to let go of the process.

I heard the tender voice again when I returned to Rivendell for a few days of silence. In the evening I curled up in an easy chair in front of a fire with a book about the Benedictines. They pause seven times a day to pray the Hours. I longed for the stability of those sacred pauses. They are like the concrete groins that protect the shoreline from erosion.

Most of my life, I have grabbed hold of each day and wrung out of it as many minutes as I could before I fell asleep exhausted. But those who kept the Hours beckoned me to loosen my grip, and let Earth's course structure the day. They invited me to welcome the dawn and pause often to notice the sun's arc. They prompted me to put everything in order as the day fades and to keep vigil in the darkness.

The Hours stirred me. One voice in me wanted to preach about them. But the other voice, the one on the periphery, wanted to live in them.

50. NECESSARY COMMAS

ONE DAY OUR WRITERS' group faced a grammatical conundrum. As usual we turned to our grammar guru, a professional editor who eats dictionaries for breakfast.

"Is this comma necessary?" we asked. When we critique each other's work, one person crosses out a comma, while the next adds one in.

I already had an answer formed in my mind and was certain I was right. But the editor hesitated and puzzled me with her answer. "That depends . . . on many things, like what the writer's trying to say." She didn't have an instant answer. She needed time to grasp the complexity before her.

Once, in a class in spiritual direction, our teacher held up a jar of pond water. She said our minds are like that water, muddied by each pebble of information that sinks to the silty bottom. We need to wait for clarity to return before we speak. When I wait that long for someone to respond, the song from Jeopardy plays in my head. I interject my thoughts long before the silt has settled. Sometimes my words are helpful, but often they're not. Then I wished I had taken more time.

Waiting seems to come naturally to some. But we are not defined by our personalities. The many different ways of being in the world reflect a wholeness found in Jesus, a wholeness that our Lord invites us to share. I don't have to lament the fact that I am not a born contemplative. As the Holy Spirit bears the fruit of patience in me, I can choose to put more commas in my life. I can learn to be still for a moment.

Whenever my mind is muddied by fears, longings, and unsolved problems and my body poised to fight or flee, I try to picture that jar of pond water. As I "quiet myself" my anxieties sink and clarity emerges: there is no place that God is not, no calamity to be faced without Jesus by my side, and nothing in all creation that can separate me from God's love.

"A well-placed comma keeps the reader from becoming confused," the editor remarked. Perhaps that is why God drops them in wherever we converse with life—at stoplights and at the gym, watching sitcoms and singing songs, when we wait in line, brush our teeth, and savor a kiss.

But I have calmed and quieted myself,
I am like a weaned child with its mother;
like a weaned child I am content.
—Psalm 131:2

51. A PAINLESS DEATH

AFTER EASTER ONE YEAR, I returned to Bowen Island for a few days to write and pray the Hours. Each morning I opened the book of Benedictine prayers that led me through the seven sacred pauses.[9]

The first one, prayed at dawn, is called "Lauds." It is full of joyous praise to our Lord who has risen in this new day. The prayers that follow invite me to join Jesus in his passion and death. "Prime" is prayed after breakfast. In this hour, the wounded Jesus is led before Pilate. At mid-morning, "Terce" describes the crowds that shout at Jesus. During the noon prayer "Sext," Jesus is nailed to the cross. In the mid-afternoon, "None" recalls how Jesus is pierced in the side with a sword. "Vespers" is prayed at sunset. In this hour, our Lord is taken down from the cross. Finally, in the dark, "Compline" is prayed: Jesus is entombed. When I wake in the night, I am invited to keep vigil with Christ until his resurrection at dawn.

I was thinking about this cycle of life, death and resurrection as I walked the labyrinth at Rivendell. Previously when I made this mini-pilgrimage, I perceived the center as the very heart of God, and the journey out felt anti-climactic. But this time, as I walked closer and closer to the center, I felt like I was entering the tomb, and the path out felt triumphant. Despite the heavy

---

[9] The phrase "seven sacred pauses" comes from the title of a book on the hours by Macrina Wiederkehr, Order of St. Benedict (O.S.B). The book I used on my retreat was *The Prymer*, translated and adapted by Robert E. Webber. I have also found *The Music of Silence* by David Steindl-Rast, O.S.B. helpful.

metaphor, I didn't experience any deep emotions at the time. It seemed as though God was walking me through dance steps without music in order to prepare me for what lay ahead. This thought made me nervous. For what death was God preparing me?

"Nothing big has happened yet," I said, when I told my spiritual director about my time away. "But something sideswiped me earlier today." I began to cry as I told her that I had been accused of being somewhat heartless.

"I'm trying to keep healthy boundaries," I said and reached for another tissue. "I can't live up to everyone's expectations, but that doesn't stop people from having them or from expressing their disappointment in me. I can't believe how painful this is."

"Could this be the death you were expecting?" she asked.

I thought for a long time. "You mean I could be dying to my need for approval?"

"Maybe that's why what happened was so painful. Death is painful."

Of course it is! I had been so preoccupied with *what* death lay ahead, it didn't occur to me that this death was going to hurt. How had I missed that?

I liked the freedom that came with letting go of living up to other people's expectations, but facing their disappointment was killing me.

"What's killing you?" my spiritual director asked.

"I hear, 'You're not acceptable,' or 'I like this about you but not that.'" I began to weep again. "And 'if you don't change, I don't want you.'"

She shook her head with empathy. "What do you hear from Jesus?"

I closed my eyes and let the character of Jesus speak to me. "He accepts me—just as I am." That thought calmed me.

Once I began to see things from Jesus' perspective, I felt a little embarrassed. "I got totally hooked by my fears. I wished I'd seen this sooner. Then I could have avoided the pain."

A smile crept across her face.

I sighed. "I'm still looking for a painless death."

"Aren't we all?"

On my way home, I stopped for a coffee. I got out my phone to check the time and found a text message sent that morning. One word: Sorry.

I appreciated the apology, but I wasn't sorry it had happened. Not sorry at all.

On each of my dyings, shed your light and your love.
—"Soul of Christ" by David L. Fleming, SJ

52. REALLY USEFUL ENGINES

Blessed are those whose strength is in you,
whose hearts are set on pilgrimage…
They go from strength to strength,
till each appears before God in Zion.
—Psalm 84:5, 7

WHEN I WAS YOUNG, I believed I could do almost anything for God, if I worked hard enough. That prospect inspired me. Now it makes me tired. I hear the same thing from my peers. Yet they also tell me they miss the glory days when they did amazing things for God. They want to know how to go "from strength to strength" to the very end. I know two people who did that and died in their sixties. But before they died, like Thomas the Tank Engine, they were Really Useful Engines.

What keeps us chugging along exhausted? Perhaps it's the thought that if we slow down, God will leave us behind. Or maybe it's because we don't experience God the way we used to. When God feels distant, we don't know what to do except fuel up and try harder.

However, on the other side of fifty, God hasn't been meeting me at the station with loads of coal. I specifically asked God to reach down from on high and lift me out of menopause, but it hasn't happened yet. I rarely get a full night's sleep. And yes, I've tried Melatonin. Instead of becoming stronger, I am getting weaker. And by the looks of things, my life will keep on going in that direction.

One Sunday I was sort of listening to the sermon when I noticed an eighty-four-year-old woman of prayer, chin on chest, soundly asleep. I wanted to wake her up and tell her to stop it or she'd get older even faster.

Since the Holy Spirit isn't helping me defy the aging process, what is God doing? I can't believe God's given up on the steamies in favor of the younger, faster diesels. Could the Spirit be encouraging us to stop trying to catch up and enter life as it is? Perhaps getting older isn't bad, just different.

The first half of my life, I went after what I wanted. I was like the Little Engine That Could. I believed that I got to the top of the mountain by hard work and determination, repeatedly telling myself, "I think I can. I think I can." Now that I am over the hill, I slide down the other side admitting, "I know I can't. I know I can't." It's not a litany of defeat, but a sigh of relief.

Actually, there are a number of things I never could do but didn't want to acknowledge it. I can't change people or make everyone happy. I can't be all things to all people. I've never been able to squeeze more hours into a day, stop bad things from happening, or find the mates to the single socks I keep in the box above the dryer.

I can't even change myself. Willpower may change my behavior for a time, but only God can transform my character.

The strength I need isn't in my body or my mind; it's in God. I go from God's strength to God's strength as I learn to trust the Spirit more. Though my Creator may feel distant, God is not gone. Though I need to rest longer, resting allows me to discover that God is right before my eyes. Though I take credit for fewer accomplishments, I discover more fears have vanished. And when I have a "mental-pause" and don't know what to say, well, I have the opportunity to become a really useful listener.

53. COME DOWN

"IF YOU KEEP ARRIVING at dinnertime, you're going to get a reputation around here," I said to my nephew.

"I think I already have one." He laughed and gave me a hug. "It's good to see you, Auntie. Mind if I use the phone in your study?"

"Go ahead."

On his way he grabbed some salsa and chips from the cupboard.

I looked at the dinner I was making and felt resentful. "I wish he would ask before he comes for dinner," I grumbled to my son. "And I wish he wouldn't help himself to everything."

Rudy put down the magazine he was reading. "Now correct me if I'm wrong, but didn't you tell him he could come over anytime and make himself at home?"

Just like that, I was caught in the disparity between who I am and who I'd like to be.

The next day I found myself in scripture. Not in the book of Esther, but in the story of Zacchaeus. Zacchaeus was the "wee little man" we sang about in Sunday School who "climbed up in the sycamore tree, for the Lord he wanted to see."

One minute I was reading the story and the next I am in it. Up in the tree, a branch arching under my sandals, I can see over the tops of people's heads. What a brilliant plan: I have the best view of Jesus. As he comes closer, I can hear what he is saying, and what he says is, "Esther, come down."

I can't believe Jesus is speaking to me. I push the leaves aside, and there he is, inches from my foot, looking up at me. My heart pounds and, before my head has a chance to protest, I shinny down the tree.

Standing next to him, I'm painfully aware of how small I am. Jesus and everyone else seem to be aware of it too. I had not expected this. I thought that when I answered Jesus' call to descend, I would somehow be elevated. I hoped I would be the last who was made first, not the other way round. How I wish I were back up in the tree, a safe distance from my shortcomings in general and my resentment and stinginess in particular.

Jesus puts his arm around my shoulder, and we walk home. The muttering, curious crowd follows.

I want Jesus to defend my sorry state, but he doesn't. Instead he announces to all the good news that salvation has come to my house, for he has come to find and restore the lost.

Sheesh. That's me he's talking about.

I lower my voice and tell Jesus I'm disappointed. He looks at me as if I've been observing life through the wrong end of the binoculars.

Then I realize why I'm disappointed. I don't want Jesus to find and restore me; I want him to find and restore my pride.

A week later my nephew dropped by again.

"I have a confession to make," I said as I followed him into the kitchen. "You know how I told you to make yourself at home? Well . . . to be honest, I'm not that comfortable with you helping yourself to things."

"Aunt Esther, I'm sorry. I had no idea." His face turned pink; he had already scooped some hummus into a bowl.

"Of course you didn't. Why would you?" I paused to gather more courage. "I didn't think it would bother me. I wish it didn't."

"That's all right. I'm glad you told me."

"Thanks for understanding," I said and gave him a hug.

"Please, have this," I said and put the bowl of hummus back into his hands. "Heidi made it and it's really good. Would you like some pita bread too?"

"You're sure?"

"Absolutely."

54. THE DIVINE REVELATION OF SIN

I WANT TO CHANGE my relationship with sin. I don't want to become blasé about my wrongdoing, but the process of recognizing and confessing my sin is, to say the least, unappealing. Realizing I've blown it is as much fun as getting hives. Who wants to know they have hurt someone or disobeyed God? I hate receiving the cold, hard facts.

Yet St. Augustine seemed to love it. He was determined to eradicate sin from his life. He kept striving for perfection to the end, even though he knew God loved him unconditionally. I would never have put those two concepts together. I assumed hyper-vigilance came from a fear of God's wrath, not from a certainty of God's love. Augustine must have had a different paradigm for sin than I do—a more compassionate one.

"Something happened yesterday that put me in a bad mood all day," I said to a friend over coffee one day. I explained what happened and then said, "I didn't even think of praying about it. What kind of contemplative forgets to pray? Instead, I spent the day nursing my fears. When I woke up this morning, I finally figured out I had done something wrong." I could barely look my friend in the eye.

"But you realized it. And it took you less than twenty-four hours. I think that's pretty good," she said. "I also think that God was with you yesterday, even while you were 'nursing your fears.' The Holy Spirit knew how you felt and was interceding for you and your situation."

Her compassion moved me to tears. It helped me to understand how Augustine could face his sin so easily: he experienced that kind of understanding from God.

There's the difference. Whenever I sin, I experience a sense of shame. What kind of contemplative forgets to pray? I had asked myself; the rhetorical answer being: a bad one. But when I forget to pray or I act unkindly, does God think I'm a bad person? I can imagine people rolling their eyes and shaking their heads at me. But I can't imagine Jesus doing that. He is with me in my guilt, sadness, and regret—and offers joy, of all things! Felix culpa!

The Latin phrase *felix culpa*, attributed to St. Augustine, means "O happy sin." Augustine used it to express the joy he felt when he discovered and confessed a sin. Apparently when he was on his deathbed, he had seven penitential psalms inscribed on the ceiling of his room. He wanted them before him as his last words. He didn't see this as a fear-based exercise but as a joy-filled opportunity. He welcomed Jesus to do what he does best: graciously forgive sins, gloriously save sinners.[10] He wanted Jesus to find and fill all the places where he was lost.

The morning before I met my friend for coffee I had read these words by Henri Nouwen, "In the light of divine Love . . . we experience God saying, 'I love you so deeply. I want to be present to you in all your "lost" places so you will know, not just your lostness, but also in how many places I long to find you.'"[11]

I'm beginning to get it. Augustine wasn't on the lookout for sin because it marred his otherwise perfect life. He was on the lookout for more places to put God's love. He wanted God in every nook and cranny of his being.

---

[10] Eugene Peterson, *Leap Over a Wall: Earthy Spirituality for Everyday Christians*. (New York, NY: Harper Collins, 1991), 237.

[11] Henri Nouwen, *From Fear to Love: Lenten Reflections on the Parable of the Prodigal Son*. (Fenton Mo: Creative Communications), 4.

55. FELIX CULPA!

IN *LEAP OVER A WALL*, Eugene Peterson encourages us to be on the lookout for our sin. Like trained bird watchers, he says we should "go looking for our sin with a certain sense of anticipation and delight; for each discovery of sin brings us to the brink of grace."[12]

Inspired by St. Augustine and his motto *felix culpa:* O Happy Sin, I decided to keep my eye out for sin. I turned my binoculars away from other peoples' lives and focused on my own.

In a conversation with two friends, I observed how well one woman listened to the other. I marveled at what she remembered from past conversations. A thought flitted by. I had said to myself, You're not a very good listener. That woman's much better at it than you are.

Right away I identified a pair of sins—judgment and envy. I didn't like discovering them, but I did like catching and confessing them before shame offered them a perch.

It isn't easy to do, but naming our sin is essential. Years ago I tried to deal with sin by emulating a saint who prayed the Jesus prayer with every breath. Jesus Christ, Son of God, have mercy on me a sinner, I had prayed, but I was afraid to fill in the blanks. I didn't want to know where I fell short of the glory of God.

But as I began to name and confess my sins, I thought of Ann Voskamp's book *A Thousand Gifts*. Voskamp set out to record a thousand gifts from God. As she gave thanks for each

---

[12] Ibid 186

one, her joy increased. In the same way, I hoped that becoming less afraid of discovering my sin would increase mine. The trick was not to let my sins condemn me. I needed to "bring them to the brink of grace" and remember that God loves us while we are in sin and is responsible for our sanctification. We are saved *and* sanctified by grace.

Just as birdsong alerts the birder, sadness is often the first sign that sin has alighted. I feel guilty. But is it true guilt or false guilt? Sin watchers need to know the difference with the same certainty that bird watchers distinguish one kind of jay from another.

While we're on the subject of discernment, it accomplishes little for sinners to say sorry for everything. I have sometimes confessed a sin that the Holy Spirit rejected. *Uh-uh, you can't count that one. That wasn't your fault.*

Birders are constantly attuned to singsong conversations in the air. They will say, "That's a chickadee" or "Oh, a meadowlark." They wait for your surprise when they say, "Hear that? That's a bald eagle." Following their example, I am trying to take some measure of delight when I spot little sins. But I don't really want to go looking "with anticipation" for the biggies. And no, I don't need any help. Besides, it isn't good to be compulsive about it.

We are to fix our eyes on Jesus, not on our sin. Avid birders have binoculars handy if they need them, but they don't go around viewing the world through them. Think of the beauty and wonder they would miss if they did. When I'm reading to my grandchildren or enjoying a delicious meal, I don't want to be thinking about anything else. I also don't go looking for my sin when I'm tired or overwhelmed by life. At those times my discernment is poor, and I am tempted to collect my sins instead of releasing them to God. Holding onto those shame-pecking sins is about as wise as holding a live chicken by the leg.

Finally, I suspect that every birder has a story about the sighting of a rare bird. If they kept score, it would be worth a hundred sightings of ordinary ones. The payoff for anyone who is brave enough to look at their own sin is the quintessential moment when they see a sinful habit that has plagued them for decades. Recognizing, owning and confessing something like that—to God and to the ones we love—is transformational.

I know that from experience. But I'm not going to tell you that story. You'll have to take my word for it.

If we confess our sins, he is faithful and just
and will forgive us our sins
and purify us from all unrighteousness.
—1 John 1:9

56. CHRIST, THE SIN-BEARER

Christ was offered once to bear the sins of many.
—Hebrews 9:28a (NKJV)

A FRIEND OF MINE is a chaplain at a forensic psychiatric hospital. He said he'd never forget the day the doctor, who taught psychiatry, invited him to come to one of his classes. He introduced the chaplain to the students and said that some of the inmates he and the chaplain worked with had killed their spouse, parents, or siblings.

"It's my job to prescribe medication that will help them recognize what they've done," the psychiatrist said and then turned to my friend. "And it's his job to help them live with it."

The chaplain was astounded. How could he possibly do that?

Though the enormity of the inmates' plight is beyond my experience, I can relate. I have committed sins that caused others to suffer.

Recently, I gave a fellow in our church some advice that squashed his fragile confidence. My intentions were well-meaning, you could hardly call advice giving a sin, but there was no mistaking how much I had hurt this man. Even though I apologized and was forgiven, it may take years before he trusts me again. Our strained Sunday morning greetings burden me still. Yet that example is minor compared to the anguish I feel when I recognize how my sins have affected my family.

I shared the chaplain's dilemma. How could I live with myself when the victim of my wrongdoing has to deal with the mess I created, in whole or in part? Conversely, how could I live with what has been done to me?

As I wrestled with this, I came across Hebrews 9:28 which reminded me that Christ is the only one able to bear sin. We are sinners, but Christ alone is the sin-bearer. For the first time, I understood that we were never created to bear sin—even our own. When we discover we have sinned, we are meant to give that sin, and its consequences, over to God.

Once we admit our wrong, Christ cleanses us from sin, and we become whiter than snow (Ps 51:7). Our sin is gone—as far away as the east is from the west (Ps. 103:12). We're no longer condemned (Ro 8:1).

Yet the damage is done. The event and its aftermath are not whisked away and forgotten. Even though we have been forgiven, we must live with the reality of what we did. This burden is too heavy to bear, so Jesus offers to bear it for us. He promises to turn mourning into dancing. But in the meantime, the only way we can look at ourselves in the mirror or keep from becoming chronically resentful is to see Jesus with us. I can picture his hand on my shoulder saying, *You can't carry this; let me.*

The morning of my fifty-fifth birthday, I remembered the day that I turned six. My older siblings declared it "Hate Esther Day." That painful memory was not hidden from God who sees all. During my morning prayer, I was invited to let the Sin-Bearer have it.

As I did, I recalled a special place where I used to go as a child. Down the road from our house, train tracks crossed over a creek that cut through fields of wheat. When I wanted to be by myself, I would sit on the concrete ledge under the tracks three yards above the stream. With my back against concrete, I'd toss stones in the water and sing songs. But as soon as I heard a train coming, I'd skedaddle. Hands over ears, heart pounding, I'd watch the hundred car train from a safe distance. I never considered staying in my concrete alcove while a train passed overhead. I'd be perfectly safe, but it was far too scary.

That morning as I continued in prayer, I pictured myself on that ledge again with Jesus. I sensed that when the next train came, he didn't want me to get up and run away. He promised to wrap himself around me and shield me from debris and fear as the rumbling weight and screeching wheels coursed overhead. He would hold me tightly until the last car was gone.

Then I realized that Jesus has been doing this for years while life, loud and terrifying, passed over me. These trains have come and gone, and they will come and go again.

A few days after my fifty-fifth birthday, a "train" did come. In prayer, I pictured myself hunkered down and protected on that concrete ledge with Jesus' arms around me. I took slow deliberate breaths and counted cars. The wheels sung: *this will pass; this will pass; this will pass.*

57. THE EVIL SIDE OF PIES

"I BOUGHT PEACHES IN the fall once," a friend said the day after I purchased twenty pounds of them at a fruit stand in the Similkameen Valley. "They were pasty and flavorless; I never made that mistake again."

The peaches were still hard, so I couldn't tell if I'd wasted my money or not. Then I realized it wouldn't be such a big deal if they ended up in the compost. If nothing else, I had supported the family that owned the orchard.

Not that long ago, I could not have made a "mistake" like that without being hounded by guilt.

I remembered Heidi's nineteenth birthday. To celebrate the day, I had made an apple and two blueberry pies. As her guests enjoyed pieces of warm pie topped with ice cream, I heard a satisfying chorus of "Mmm, pie."

But the next day, I discovered the evil side of pies. They had maliciously spewed yellow and purple lava all over my non-self-cleaning oven. If only I hadn't baked three pies at once. If only I'd put more vents in the top crusts or placed the pies on a cookie sheet. What a mess.

I got a can of oven cleaner and shook it hard. I held my breath and sprayed the oven's surfaces and let the door slam against the fumes. A few hours later, I returned to find five spots on the kitchen floor. Each spot resembled a cartoon bullet hole: a blood-black circle surrounded by tiny splash marks. I scrubbed the floor to no avail; oven cleaner had burned holes in the linoleum.

I laid newspaper down in front of the oven, something I should have done before I cleaned it. Wasn't that the advice I gave my kids? Kneeling before the oven, I accepted my penance and cleaned to an internal litany of should have, could have, didn't.

As I worked, I thought of Rudy, who would soon turn twenty-two, and Heidi. For the next hour, my insecurity as a parent ganged up and pelted me with accusations. I felt responsible for many of the difficulties they had in their lives.

I stood up and rinsed out the cleaning cloth. As I watched the dirty water circle down the drain, I wished my black feelings would disappear with it. I closed the oven and balled up the newspaper. The five dark stars—a permanent Cassiopeia—remained.

How I wished I could go back in time and do things differently, not just with the oven, but also with my kids. How I wished I had overcome the bad habits that had hurt them. For a long time, I stood at the sink and soaked and squeezed the blackened cloth. Then I turned off the faucet, sank to the floor, and wept.

Eventually I wiped my eyes. I fingered the burned scars on the floor and prayed, Well, Jesus, now what? I can't undo the past; it looks like the damage is done.

I sat for a while in silence, then I remembered what Heidi had said after the party. I was loading the dishwasher when she said, "That was the best birthday ever." Despite the evil side of pies and their maker, Heidi had hugged me and declared, "You rock, Mom." Those were her exact words.

Heidi turned twenty-six last week. Now I have to look hard to see the burn marks on the floor. They're barely detectable.

When the peaches were finally ripe, I cut into one and handed a piece to Fred. "The moment of truth," I said.

We both agreed: it was the most delicious peach we had ever tasted.

58. WEEDS OF INSECURITY

"Do you want us to go and pull them up?" the servants asked the owner of the wheat field.

"No," he replied, "wait until the harvest."

Groan. Whenever I read the parable of the wheat and the weeds, I'd like a different answer. That's because I want to be rid of the weeds that were planted in my childhood.

I grew up in rural Ontario, the middle child of five siblings. During those days of building forts and being spies, many beliefs were seeded in my mind and heart. Years passed and those seeds sprouted and grew, wheat and weeds together.

Report cards called me "conscientious." I did what I was told and never made a fuss—earning me the rhythm sticks instead of bells or cymbals every time. Though I was a good kid, I feared I was never good enough. Insecurity entangled whatever I did.

How I tried to uproot my fears with scripture and accomplishments. As soon as I thought I'd licked those insecurities, they would spring to life again. I kept waiting for the harvest, and decades later I'm still waiting.

But I think those weeds are scrawnier than they used to be. I don't get knocked down as often, and I recover more quickly when faced with loss or disappointment. Perhaps, like God's kingdom, the harvest has come and is still coming. I know that God will completely uproot my fears when Christ comes again, but the Gardener has done a lot of work already, especially since I began praying in silence.

As I rested in God's presence, I tried not to fidget. Inevitably

I'd say, Okay, I'm here. Is there anything you want to say to me? Then I'd brace myself for the truth.

I love you, is all I seemed to hear.

Anything else? Anything you want me to do? Any sin I should confess or habit to work on?

Just receive my love.

Day after day the same message came to me. Eventually I felt loved and cherished. I began to trust that God would look after me and bring something good out of whatever might happen. Even shingles.

A couple of years ago when I got shingles, I suffered through weeks of discomfort, fatigue, and embarrassment. Apparently the chickenpox virus, which causes shingles, lies dormant in your body until more stress than you can handle wears you down. I had to admit, yet again, that I couldn't be the pastor, friend, or mother I wanted to be.

This reminded me of a time when I felt like my mother wasn't all I wished she was. I carried that hurt for thirty years. But as I suffered through shingles and accepted my own limitations, I was able to see my mother in a more compassionate light. I forgave her, though there really wasn't anything to forgive. But when I did, God plucked a thirty-year-old weed.

With that resentment gone, I began to see the wheat that grew tall and golden. Good memories returned. I remembered my mother braiding my hair and taking a photo of my sister and me in the gingham dresses she had made us: Sylvie's was blue with cross-stitched tulips on it, and mine was green with baby chicks.

I also remembered the time I was in a car accident and my pelvis was broken. When I got out of hospital, my mother left my dad to fend for himself and flew from Ontario to B.C. to look after us. I was on bed rest; Fred worked full-time; Rudy attended kindergarten half days; Heidi was toilet training, and our little dog, Harry, needed to be walked. She took care of us all and made Linzer Torte too.

I am thankful you uprooted my resentment, I told God, but why did it take you thirty years?

Then I pictured my heavenly Gardener crouching down and working in my garden. I got the impression God isn't bothered by those pesky weeds half as much as I am.

59. GIFTS

every morning
you bring gifts
practical   precise
perplexing   profound
revealing something
    of you
    and me

in summer
I wake early
just to see what's new
in winter
they collect
unopened till
spring rouses curiosity

some I keep
line them up
show them off
others take up space
get in the way
and don't endear you
to my friends

I throw them out
then
in the night
get dressed
and retrieve them
from the trash

it was easy to call them all
gifts
until a box arrived
with no return address

    and changed

        everything

I closed it up
pushed it away

    you pushed it back

like a couple of kids
we pushed it
back and forth
and back and forth

I don't want it
I yelled
I know what's inside

    so do I
    you said
    joy and life

in this box?

    that
made me want to lift the lid
    and look again

60. NOTICE WHAT YOU NOTICE

DAILY I ASK THE blessed Trinity to lead me deeper into God's transforming love. How do I expect that prayer to be answered?

When I was a child, as soon as I sent a letter in the mail, I checked the mailbox daily for a reply. But when I grew up, I sent prayers heavenward and walked away feeling a little ticked off with God's silence. I never noticed that God constantly answers my mail. I have stepped on it, brushed it aside, and used the back of it for grocery lists.

"Notice what you notice," a Jesuit priest said to me while leading me through the Ignatian Spiritual Exercises. "What stands out for you when you think back over your day? Could God be working in these things to love and transform you?"

I began to notice what I noticed, collecting my findings like clues to a mystery.

In early April I noticed that there were still no leaves on the maple trees. For a second I thought the trees might be dead. The cherry blossoms had already come and gone. It's kind of embarrassing to admit, but for the first time in my life, I realized I had never paid attention to how leaves bud and grow. I watched them turn color and wave goodbye in autumn, but I never welcomed them in spring.

Notice what you notice.

One Saturday Fred and I watched *The Best Exotic Marigold Hotel*. I noticed that I loved the way the details were woven into the plot. I noticed the quotable line in the movie, "Everything will be all right in the end. So if it's not all right, it is not yet the end." And I noticed, with a certain degree of discomfort, the convicting words Mr. Ainslie said to his wife, Jean. He said, "Can you hear yourself? Can you? Do you have any idea what a terrible person you have become? All you give out is this endless negativity, a refusal to see any kind of light and joy, even when it's staring you in the face."

Why did I notice that part? I suppose because I never want to be like Mrs. Ainslie, a hardened, blind, spoilsport. I didn't really want to see how I might be heading in that direction. I let this noticing float away.

The next day as if on cue, I became Jean Ainslie—and at a church event no less—when things weren't going my way.

A few of us were preparing lunch after church to honor two dozen volunteers. Before church, the fellow I asked to be in charge chatted with one person then another. He seemed unconcerned that there were a million things to do in a limited amount of time. I fretted, frowned, and fussed. Meanwhile another man was making coffee and watching us. "Relax," he said and put his hand on my back. "Let him do it his way. What's the worst that can happen?"

I didn't want to think about it. I prepared myself for a chaotic, frantic end, but the fellow in charge, Mr. Pull-It-Off-at-the-Last-Minute, soared above my negativity and pulled it off at the last minute. The meal was a success.

After the dishes were done, I went home and put my feet up. As I sat there drinking my coffee, I recalled the coffee maker's question. What was the worst that could have happened? Not a spoiled meal or dissatisfied guests, but me—becoming Mrs. Ainslie!

Notice what you notice.

I like happy endings and how the things I notice contribute to the plot. Despite my whiny negativity, it was all right in the end. God's hand was on my back, and a new way of being was budding.

*And we know that in all things
God works for the good of those who love him,
who have been called according to his purpose.*
—Romans 8:28

61. HOLY INDIFFERENCE

OFTEN WHEN I PREPARE sermons, I like to read them over to Fred the day before I give them. However one Saturday, events conspired against me. It was four o'clock in the afternoon before we got a few minutes together while watching our grandchildren at the park. Even then, they interrupted us several times before they finally settled down to play in the sandbox.

No sooner had I resumed reading my sermon aloud, when a woman who sat nearby asked, "Aren't you from the church down the street?"

"Yes," I said. Couldn't she see I was trying to work?

I knew she was more important than my work, and that I needed to stop and chat with her. But I couldn't handle one more interruption.

St. Ignatius believed that God gives all things—including meaningful work—to help us love God and our neighbors. But if we hold onto these gifts too tightly, like I did that afternoon in the park, they bind us. An inordinate attachment to work or any other good thing occupies our attention and distracts us from opportunities to give or receive love. The remedy, Ignatius taught, is to ask God for the grace we need to hold all things with "holy indifference."

Weeks later I was biking home from an appointment. My route took me past a bakery that makes delicious gluten free bread. I had a pile of work waiting for me at home and wondered if I should take the time to pick up a loaf for Hadrian. But on this day, the urgency of work didn't tip the scales in its favor.

"This bread sure was a hit at our daughter's wedding," I said to the baker who owned the store.

"I'll bet you're glad that's behind you. Weddings are expensive and a ton of work," he said, smiling.

His comment surprised me. Over the years, I have tried to engage him in conversation but rarely got more than a word out of him, never mind a smile.

"All my kids are happily married," he said and went on to tell me he had once lived in a small town up north. "My wife died giving birth to our third child. There I was with a newborn and two preschoolers. I quit my job to raise the kids. A Polish woman lived next door; she helped me. My daughter still writes to her. She's got to be ancient now; she was old then!"

I shook my head, amazed.

"Not many men raised kids themselves in those days," he said and smiled as he handed me my change.

I was honored to hear his story. Days later I continued to savor our conversation. It reminded me of Frances, the writer in *Under the Tuscan Sun,* and her old, Italian neighbor. Day after day she waved at him without a response. Then finally one day he gave her a nod.

I was glad I went into the bakery and thankful for the grace that allowed me to do it.

62. STONES

Each of you is to take up a stone on his shoulder . . . to serve as a sign among you. In the future, when your children ask you, "What do these stones mean?" tell them that the flow of the Jordan was cut off before the ark of the covenant of the LORD. When it crossed the Jordan, the waters of the Jordan were cut off. These stones are to be a memorial to the people of Israel forever. —Joshua 4:5-7

    at the end of the day
    all we have are
        stories
    like the stones the Israelites found
    in the riverbed
    when the water was
    held back

    a Voice inside you said
        pick this one
        carry it on your shoulder
        remember what happened

    when you tell me that story
    I feel the weight of it
    our eyes meet
    we both know:
        the Lord has been here

63. A STILL SMALL VOICE

IT WAS HER CRYING that stopped me.

I was biking through an industrial section of Burnaby when I saw her standing in front of a warehouse with an old bike in one hand and a large plastic bag of empties in the other. She was about forty years old, painfully thin, and toothless.

I walked my bike over to her. "Are you okay?"

Startled, she dropped the bag of cans and bottles.

"Are you all right?" I asked again, even more gently than I had before.

"No . . . I don't know." She wiped her nose with the back of her hand. "I feel . . . faint."

"When did you eat last?"

"This morning, I think."

"I can't see," she said and started crying again.

"Maybe I can help you," I said. "What's your name?"

"Cheryl. I'm waiting for someone. He said he was going to meet me here. Do you see anyone?"

"No one. What's his name?"

She grasped her forehead with a dirt-encrusted hand and shook her head. "I don't know," she moaned. "He said he'd meet me here." She began to walk away.

Afraid she'd wander into traffic, I called 911.

"Can you stay with her until the ambulance arrives?" was the last question dispatch asked.

"Yes," I said.

"Help is coming, Cheryl."

"I've got to find him." She walked toward the street.

"Let's wait here until the ambulance comes," I said and stood in her way.

Cheryl wandered into a patch of tall grass. "Where are you?" she called. When she came out, her arms were pricked and bleeding. Then she headed for the street again.

"We need to wait here." I held out my hand to stop her. She pushed against it.

When she relaxed a little, I took her hand in mine. "Cheryl, the ambulance is coming. They're coming to help you because you're precious. You're very precious to God."

The moment I heard the sirens, she squeezed my hand. The blaring got louder; she squeezed tighter. As four men converged upon us, Cheryl began to have a seizure.

"Let's lay her down," a fireman said and pried her hand from mine. "How long has she been like this?"

"It happened when you got here," I said.

The ambulance arrived shortly after that. The attendants asked me a questions that I didn't know the answers to. Tenderly they put her on a stretcher and took her away. Meanwhile a fireman got out a clipboard and took down my name and address and asked me more questions.

"I'm glad I called 911," I said.

"We are too. Thanks for stopping," the fireman said and tucked the clipboard under his arm. "You did your good deed for the day."

Then they were gone, Cheryl's bike and bag of empties abandoned.

A good deed? Is that what it was?

When I arrived home, I called Progressive Housing Society and left a message letting them know what had happened. They likely knew Cheryl and the man she was waiting for.

That night at our contemplative group, I told them what happened.

"Good thing you were there," one said.

"You likely saved her life," said another.

The next day I heard back from Progressive Housing. They knew Cheryl and had contacted her friend to let him know she was in ICU. I hoped to visit Cheryl, but between one thing and another it never happened. After a few days, she was released from hospital.

Two Wednesdays later, we were having a barbecue instead of soup to celebrate Canada Day. Word about the lunch had gotten around, and more than the regulars attended. Cheryl was one of them.

I didn't see her at first; she had her back to me. But she recognized my voice, got up from her chair and turned around. She looked transformed: combed hair, clean clothes, teeth in, and eyesight restored.

"You're my angel," she said and hugged me fiercely.

"Cheryl, it's good to see you."

"Thank you for what you did." She was crying and hugged me again and again. "You saved my life."

I thought about what happened for months. When I talked to friends about it, I said anyone would have done what I did. But they disagreed. One told me that recently a hundred people had walked by a man in distress at a Skytrain station. No one helped him, and he died as a result.

I didn't feel like I was one in a hundred. I could have easily kept on riding. It disturbed me how easily I could have done that. I had no idea when I stopped what was going to happen. But God knew.

Why didn't God shout down from on high and say, "Esther, you have to do something, NOW." If someone is in danger you'd think God would communicate more urgently.

I mulled it over until finally I realized: God didn't need a megaphone. God knew that her crying would stop me.

Then God said to Elijah, "Go out, and stand on the mountain before the LORD." And behold, the LORD passed by, and a great and strong wind tore into the mountains and broke the rocks in pieces before the LORD, but the LORD was not in the wind; and after the wind an earthquake, but the LORD was not in the earthquake; and after the earthquake a fire, but the LORD was not in the fire; and after the fire a still small voice. So it was, when Elijah heard it, that he wrapped his face in his mantle and went out and stood in the entrance of the cave.

—1Kings 19: 11-13 (NKJV)

64. BEGINNING AGAIN

I CAN STILL PICTURE him in his Italian leather shoes as he stood on a beached log. He wore a buttoned-up shirt and stiff new jeans. His forehead was pinched as he scanned the shoreline, watching and waiting.

"You from around here?" he had asked that day as Fred and I finished our picnic supper on Rialto Beach in Washington State.

"No. Canada," Fred replied. "Vancouver."

"I don't know what house prices are like where you live, but they're substantiality higher in Seattle than they are in Michigan." The man smoothed his grey hair, tucked his hands in his pockets, and sat down on a nearby log. "My son got transferred here last year, so my daughters and I have come out for a visit. This trip was their idea. Probably thought it would take my mind off the divorce, but it hasn't really."

His unexpected revelation fluttered into my heart like a wounded sparrow. I looked into his sad eyes and waited. After a long pause, he asked Fred what he did for a living.

Fred told him he was a landscaper.

"I worked for the government, in national defense," the man said. "This isn't how I imagined heading into retirement. We were married less than a year. Now the lawyers are sorting everything out. In the meantime, she's living in my house, using the new car. I had to sell the RV and move in with my youngest daughter."

He looked out at the surf then at me. "My first wife and I were together for thirty-one years. The day after she turned fifty-three, we found out she had a brain tumor. The doctor told us she didn't have long to live. A few months, maybe a year with chemotherapy. Things appeared hopeful for a while; then she got another tumor. When she passed away, I didn't know what to do with myself. The kids were grown up and on their own.

"Then I met my second wife. I guess you could say she swept me off my feet. She's half my age, but it didn't matter to her." His wistful expression turned into a grimace. "My daughters saw right through her, warned me to be careful."

He shook his head. "When her car broke down, I bought her a new one; I paid her son's medical bills. I trusted her, and all the while she was cheating on me. She got fired from her job for having sex with her co-worker in the restroom, for God's sake."

He stopped speaking as two women approached. "Care to come for a walk, Dad?" one asked.

"No," he said. "I don't want to ruin my shoes. You go ahead."

I wondered if his daughters would cajole him into going with them, but they didn't. "All right," they said and picked up their conversation without glancing back

"I've probably told you more than you want to know," he said.

"It's okay," I reassured him, then asked. "Have you found any peace in this?"

"I can't stop thinking about it." He pressed his hands against the log, almost getting up then sitting back down. "If I could get angry at her, I'd feel better. But I still love her. That's the crazy part." He stood up and brushed the sand from his shoes.

"Do you mind if I pray for you?" I asked.

"That would be nice." He bowed his head.

I closed my eyes and listened for the right words to come as the waves inhaled. I thanked God for being with him and asked God to comfort him and bring something good out of it all.

When the man opened his eyes again, he seemed to be returning from somewhere far away, as if for a moment he had forgotten why he was upset.

"Thank you," he said. "I hope you enjoy your vacation."

"You take care of yourself," Fred said and shook his hand.

Later Fred and I went for a walk on the beach and I spotted the man again scanning the shoreline for his daughters, gazing out to sea for answers. I waved, but he looked past us.

Further along we saw "I ♥ Jesus" written in the sand by a youthful, confident hand. Soon the rising tide would wash the message out to sea along with every footprint and sandcastle on the beach.

In the morning, we will all begin again.

65. WATER

water
crystal clear
from mountain stream
flows in Nile   Ganges
creek
where salmon spawn
and toddlers wade

water
bottled   bought and sold
(two for one till Tuesday)
carbonated   infiltrated
emancipated
done

water
found   cherished   drawn
from village well
and carried home
sloshing   spills
in crevassed ground
to seed and dream
eternal

water
blessed   begins
and rests
poured out stretched
to rise again
with tidal breath

66. GATHERED HOME

JOHNNY COULD HARDLY CONTAIN his joy. "Do you know what happened to me yesterday?"

Johnny comes to the church for soup on Wednesdays. His home is a carefully concealed tent in the woods. He is a small, weatherworn fifty-year-old with big, curly hair. In the past, he told me that when he rides the bus or walks down the street, mothers sometimes take one look at him and move their children to the other side. Incidents like these can ignite his anger and make him swear, pace, and clench his fists. But he is not angry today.

"Yesterday, I got filled up, man," he said excitedly. "I was at a park in the West End, and I ran into this old friend of mine. She was babysitting her granddaughter. I hadn't seen that little girl for a while. I didn't even think she would remember me. But when she saw me, she came running. I got down on my knees like this." He knelt down and spread out his arms. "She ran right into my arms. She had a big grin on her face and spoke in a full sentence. At three years old! She said, 'I missed you!' I tell you that filled me up with good energy."

That story filled me up too. It seemed like God had run into his arms and hugged him. Finally.

Johnny needs filling up. Daily he struggles to survive against the elements and wild creatures—on four legs and two—that gnaw at his hope.

Two months before that loving embrace, Johnny had gone to collect his stash of empty cans and bottles and stumbled upon a man who had hanged himself. The body was still warm. Johnny dropped everything and ran onto the street to get help. He stopped eight cars before he found someone willing to call 911.

When I saw Johnny the Wednesday after it happened, he was in tears. "Esther, I need you to pray for me. I can't eat; I can't sleep. I keep seeing that man's face. Pray for me; pray for all of us. Now, please."

Slowly Johnny recovered the energy he had lost from that traumatizing experience. When I heard how that little girl's hug affected him, I wanted his joy to last forever.

Two weeks later I was sitting down with a bowl of soup when Johnny arrived. He walked stiffly and had lost weight. He bent down and whispered in my ear, "Three guys followed me, stalked me. I turned around and told them to F off, that there's a law against stalking people. Then one of them grabbed me and threw me down. They kicked the shit out of me. I ended up in hospital with three broken ribs."

He sat down beside me to finish the story. "And the cops? They didn't do nothing, even though I had a description of the car. I'm going to have to do the cops' job for them. I'll find the shits that did this, and they're going to get what they deserve."

I glanced around at the others sitting at the table. They too were shocked to hear what had happened to Johnny.

For days I kept thinking about him. How I wished I could rearrange the stories of his life, so that the bad things happened before the little girl hugged him, and only good ones followed.

But while I am wishing, God is acting. Scripture says, "For this is what the Sovereign Lord says: 'I myself will search for my sheep and look after them'"

And that includes Johnny.

God never stops. Never will. Right now God is gathering the scattered and bringing us all home.

For this is what the Sovereign LORD *says,*
"I myself will search for my sheep and look after them.
I will rescue them from all the places
where they were scattered on a day of clouds and darkness.
I will search for the lost and bring back the strays.
I will bind up the injured and strengthen the weak."
—Ezekiel 34:11, 12, 16

67. WATER II

I am poured out like water.—Psalm 22:14a

will I
be poured out? am I
available? can I
be used overlooked undervalued?

as I
wonder
will I? am I? can I?
I am
dropped
and
splatter
everywhere

outside myself
I devise ways
I could have fallen
without
falling apart

while you
collect my
droplets in the mist

68. JOURNEY'S END

> *Here I raise mine Ebenezer;*
> *hither by thy help I'm come;*
> *and I hope, by thy good pleasure,*
> *safely to arrive at home.*
> —Robert Robinson

THE LAST TEN YEARS of my pilgrimage bear witness of how tenderly God has cared for me. God attended to my insecurity, supplied me with compassion for myself and others, widened my view of salvation, and transformed me from a compulsive workaholic to a (slightly) more relaxed contemplative. Love is patient; love is kind.

One thing I learned in the process of writing this book is how important it is to raise our Ebenezers. I hope you will treasure your stories and tell them. Then others will feel the weight of what has happened and recognize God's presence.

Life continues, as do my stories. Eventually, at the end of 2014, I stopped doing half of what I had been doing and left paid ministry at New Life Community Church. You can read about it on my blog, *An Everyday Pilgrim*, which I started in July 2013 when I finished writing this book.

I leave you with one of my favorite posts called, "Night Crossing." It is about the first time I tried praying with my imagination.

I put down my cup of tea and settled myself cross-legged on the couch in the afternoon sun. Heidi was napping in her crib and Rudy at kindergarten.

I closed my eyes and pictured myself at the bow of Kimmeridge, the first sailboat we owned. Fred was at the helm and our little ones asleep. The soft winds filled the mainsail and jib; the night sky was clear and the salt air cool. I zipped up my fleece and rested my forearms on the lifelines. My bare feet dangled over the side not far from the water. The only sounds came from the slosh of the waves and ting-ting of the rigging.

I was alone and then I wasn't. Jesus, looking like he did in the pictures with long hair and a white robe, sat right beside me.

I swallowed, took a deep breath and said, "Hi."

"Hello," he said. "Nice night."

"Yes, it is."

This was my big chance. I could ask Jesus anything I wanted. I gazed up at the Big Dipper and the crescent moon and remembered that Jesus was with God in the beginning. Through him all things were created.

"What were you thinking about when you made the moon and the stars?" I asked.

"What was I thinking about?" Jesus turned to face me. "I was thinking of the night you and I would be sitting here together looking at them."

My heart thumped in my throat and a tear slid down my cheek. I never guessed he was going to say that.

When I opened my eyes, the world was as it was before. My tea was still warm and Heidi still asleep.

Would she notice when she woke up? And when I picked up Rudy from school or welcomed Fred home from work, would they see that I was not the same person I was when they left?

On the wings of the wind, You did come.
—Psalm 18:10
Nan C. Merrill, *Psalms for Praying: An Invitation to Wholeness*

ACKNOWLEDGEMENTS

I'M THANKFUL THAT GOD set my heart on pilgrimage, and didn't send me off alone. Many have travelled with me, and they fill my heart with gratitude

I can't imagine where I would be without the communities of New Life Community Church, SoulStream, and Tri-Cities Imago Dei or my spiritual directors: Sister Marilyn, Petra Anderson, Karen Webber, and Father Elton Fernandes.

Embedded in the pages of this book are the encouragement, critique and inspiration of Eileen Kernaghan and the Kyle Writers' Group, Nancy Bailey, Marina Belanger, Heather Hiebert, Wendy Holland, Jean and Steve Imbach, Jeff and Joy Imbach, Wanda Mulholland, Jayne Schmidt, and Wilma van der Leek. Thank you, Doug and Karen, for giving me retreat space to finish the book; Jeff, for writing the foreword; and Luci Shaw and Rob Des Cotes for your endorsements.

I am especially grateful for my husband, Fred (whose first gift to me thirty-six years ago was a copy of the Canadian Writers' Market), and our family: Rudy, Corinne, and Hannah; and Heidi, Jeremy and Hadrian. Thank you for your support, patience, and love. I also thank my parents, Max and Heidi, and my siblings and their families for their love throughout the years.

I thank God that I am surrounded with such a great cloud of witnesses—past and present—who have descended the spiral staircase within and passed their stories on to us.

ABOUT THE AUTHOR

Esther Hizsa lives in Burnaby, B.C., with her husband, Fred. She has a Master of Divinity degree from Regent College, Vancouver, B.C. and worked for over twenty years as an associate pastor—first in the United Church of Canada and then in the Canadian Reformed Church in America. She offers spiritual direction (trained through SoulStream) and co-facilitates SoulStream's spiritual formation course, Living from the Heart. Her writing has been published in *Journey toward Home: Soul Travel from Advent to Lent* (edited by Kristin Carroccino and Christine Sine); *Pacific Yachting* and *Mennonite Herald* magazines; and various blogs, including her own: *An Everyday Pilgrim*. She and Fred have two children and two grandchildren.

Visit *An Everyday Pilgrim* at www.estherhizsa.com

Made in the USA
Charleston, SC
04 December 2015